SOCIETY OF ASIAN NORTH AMERICAN CHRISTIAN STUDIES
JOURNAL #2 (SUMMER 2010)

Papers from the Asian American Equipping Symposium,
"Living Out the Gospel: Asian American Perspectives and Contributions"
November 2 – 3, 2009
Co-sponsored by the Institute for the Study of Asian American Christianity (ISAAC) and
Fuller Theological Seminary

	PREFACE	3
	Articles	
YOUNG LEE HERTIG	**INTRODUCTION:** *Reflections on the Inaugural Asian American Equipping Symposium*	7
JONATHAN TRAN	**FIRST KEYNOTE PRESENTATION:** *Why Asian American Christianity has no future: The over against, leaving behind, and separated from of Asian American Christian identity*	13
JONATHAN TRAN	**SECOND KEYNOTE PRESENTATION:** *Why Asian American Christianity is the future: Holding it together in yellow Christianity*	37
MIYOUNG YOON HAMMER	**RESPONSE #1**	57
CHARLENE JIN LEE	**RESPONSE #2**	63
JONATHAN TRAN	**RESPONSE #3**	69
KEN FONG	**RESPONSE #4**	75
RICHARD MOUW	**RESPONSE #5**	81
YOUNG LEE HERTIG	**AFTERWORD:** *Imagining Asian American Theological Formation and Social Capital*	87
	Book Reviews	
ANAND VEERARAJ	Kunt A. Jacobsen and Selva J. Raj, eds., *South Asian Christian Diaspora: Invisible Diaspora in Europe and North America*	95
AMOS YONG	Elaine Howard Ecklund, *Korean American Evangelicals: New Models for Civic Life*	99
RUSSELL JEUNG	Sharon Kim, *A Faith of Our Own: Second Generation Spirituality in Korean American Churches*	103
URIAH Y. KIM	Randall C. Bailey, Tat-siong Benny Liew, and Fernando F. Segovia (eds.), *They were All Together in One Place? Toward Minority Biblical Criticism*	107

THE SOCIETY OF ASIAN NORTH AMERICAN CHRISTIAN STUDIES JOURNAL

An inter-disciplinary, scholarly exploration of Asian North American Christianity

SANACS is a program of the Institute for the Study of Asian American Christianity (ISAAC)

Membership Subscriptions, address changes, advertising and business correspondence should be sent to:
Institute for the Study of Asian American Christianity (ISAAC)
6001 Castlebrook Drive, Castro Valley, CA 94552
(510) 962-5584.

Postmaster send address changes to:
SANACS Journal (ISAAC)
6001 Castlebrook Drive, Castro Valley, CA 94552.

Copyright © 2010 by the Society of Asian North American Christian Studies

All rights reserved. No part of this publication may be reproduced, stored in a retrieval system, or transmitted in any form or by any means, electronic, mechanical, photocopying, recording, or otherwise, without the prior permission of the Institute for the Study of Asian American Christianity (ISAAC).

Editor: Russell Yee

Please send submission inquires to ryee@isaacweb.org
See more detailed submission guidelines at the back

Interior layout by Daniel Chou

Institute for the Study of Asian American Christianity (ISAAC)
6001 Castlebrook Drive
Castro Valley CA 94552
http://isaacweb.org

Preface

For this second edition of the Society of Asian North American Christian Studies Journal, we are pleased to feature papers from the inaugural Asian American Equipping Symposium (AAES). This November 2009 event, titled *"Living Out the Gospel: Asian American Perspectives and Contributions,"* was co-sponsored by the Institute for the Study of Asian American Christianity (ISAAC) and Fuller Theological Seminary.

We are especially pleased that the AAES event combined full scholarly inquiry with wide-ranging concerns for ministry leadership needs. This intersection of academics and the church is precisely where ISAAC's work is focused.

By student enrollment and faculty size, ISAAC's co-sponsor for the AAES is the largest seminary in the world. It is also quite probably where the largest number of Asian North American seminary students have matriculated both presently and cumulatively to date. That such an inaugural event took place in such a setting with such a partnership is a measure of both the growing importance of Asian North American Christianity and the still-nascent stage of this urgent and vital work.

This volume includes both keynote addresses by Jonathan Tran plus five responses, all this framed by reflections from ISAAC's Southern California Director, Young Lee Hertig. She was the overall leader in planning this event. Her personal efforts and friendships enabled the collaboration with Fuller, particularly her direct work with President Richard Mouw. She also assembled the manuscripts and did the initial editing for this publication. For her initiative, vision, leadership, and boundless energy we can all be thankful.

For the next two editions of the SANACS Journal, we are especially interested in submissions in the areas of Biblical studies and in Ethics in the context of Asian North American Christianity. But we encourage submissions in all academic fields, as well as relevant book reviews. Please see the Manuscript Submission Guidelines in the back.

Russell Yee

王乃基　關以琳
Rev. Johnny & Elim Wong
3116, 115 Street,
Edmonton, Alberta
Canada, T6J 3H8

王乃基　　閻以琳
Rev. Johnny & Elim Wong
3116, 115 Street,
Edmonton, Alberta
Canada, T6J 3H8

Articles

Reprinted with permission from *Fuller Focus*, Winter 2010

Asian American Leadership Symposium Held

Can Asian American churches do well considering what they've left behind? If they order their lives by first leaving behind their pasts, what gets lost in the transition?" These were two of many questions posed by Jonathan Tran, assistant professor of theological ethics at Baylor University, at the "Asian American Leadership Equipping Symposium" held at Fuller's Pasadena campus. The event, centered on the theme "Living Out the Gospel: Asian American Contributions and Challenges," offered time for learning and connection between Asian American theologians and ministry practitioners.

The symposium, sponsored by the Institute for the Study of Asian American Christianity (ISAAC) and Fuller's Office of Alumni/ae and Church Relations and Office for Urban Initiatives, featured lectures from Dr. Tran along with an address by President Mouw, panel responses, breakout sessions, and worship times.

"The Asian American church has the ability to remind Christianity that it is not at home in America," Tran said. "Rather like Asian immigrants, Christians come from another place and are on their way to another place. Though they live here, this is not their home." The Asian American church can help transform Christianity as a whole, he declared, "because it will allow the church to more fully enter into the fullness of God's gathered body, which is not yellow or white or black, but indeed yellow *and* white *and* black, holding together that which only God's church can hold together."

INTRODUCTION
Reflections on the Inaugural Asian American Equipping Symposium

BY **YOUNG LEE HERTIG**
INSTITUTE FOR THE STUDY OF ASIAN AMERICAN CHRISTIANITY (ISAAC)

The November 2-3, 2009 Asian American Equipping Symposium was a major milestone in the emerging partnership between ISAAC-Southern California and Fuller Theological Seminary. May I offer some reflections on my personal journey as it led to this event.

When I enrolled in seminary in St. Paul, Minnesota in January 1981, I became compelled to explore several questions, most notably, "Why are Asian American Christian experiences excluded from the theological curriculum?" As every class took students to Europe, I wondered if there was even an American theology, let alone an Asian American one. Since day one, I began a quest to see how these excluded voices could be incorporated in the theological curriculum. Clearly, the entire theological menu was of European taste, cooked by European-American chefs with their choice of ingredients. Somehow, non-Europeans like me were to remain forever a guest at the table they prepared. It troubled me deeply, and I decided to learn more about the dynamics of the gospel and culture. In a missiology class taught by a Fuller alumus and professor, I began reading books written by Fuller missiology faculty, and for the first time, I found some affirmation for my questions. I went on to check out Fuller and met my wonderful mentor, Paul G. Hiebert, who, being a third generation missionary to India, could sympathize with generational and worldview clashes within the Korean American immigrant church. From this point, I devoured multidisciplinary missiology that integrated theology, culture, and psychology which Fuller Seminary uniquely offered.

Three decades later, I realized Asian American seminarians still confront some of the same questions and issues! Asian American consciousness has not entered into the theological palace despite Asian Americans becoming the largest constituency among the racial minorities in the student population at major seminaries. Still, the majority of the seminary classes take students back to Europe exclusively. As a result, like a tree without roots, Asian American seminarians find it difficult and burdensome to stand firm when the winds of politics blow their way. Consequently, in the 1990s, many of them departed from ministry, part of the phenomenon that Helen Lee described as the "Silent Exodus."[1]

In general, first generation immigrant church pastors do not mentor younger generation English-speaking pastors due to a number of reasons: 1) the busy schedule of immigrant church; 2) the linguistic inferiority by the first generation pastors; and 3) worldview differences. The seminary's color-blind curriculum inadequately prepares young Asian American pastors for ministering in Asian American church contexts. The color-blind approach to theology and bible in seminary education exacerbates Asian American, says Tim Tseng:

> There is no doubt in my mind that the "colorblind mandate" has had a devastating impact on Asian American evangelicals. It exacerbates our intergenerational gaps, separates us from the neediest Asian Americans, and leaves us feeling worthless in both the American and global contexts.[2]

The task of connecting theological equipping to Asian American contexts cannot be undertaken by one faculty member in one institution. Instead, it requires multi-levels of collaborative teamwork from both pastoral contexts and theological institutions. I can write from my own teaching experiences as a full-time faculty member at mainstream institutions. I was forced to put my passion on the backburner due to the daily institutional tasks required of me, which included serving on up to four committees as the only one without another woman of color to delegate. For reasons such as these, the Institute for the Study of Asian American Christianity (ISAAC) was formed in part to help equip Asian American equippers by Asian American scholars and pastors.

In 2005, Rev. Dr. Joshua Lee, general secretary of the National Korean Presbyterian Council of the Presbyterian Church USA and I conducted a listening session with the Korean American seminarians at Fuller Theological Seminary. Upon the conclusion of the session, ISAAC's mission of *Equip the Equippers* became more solidified. When observing and analyzing diverse Asian American populations, I have discovered that a rich social capital exists. The Asian American community's assets, resources, and talents per capital are quite impressive. However,

---

1   Helene Lee, "NEWS: Silent Exodus *Can the East Asian church in America reverse the flight of its next generation?* Additional reporting by Ted Olsen, Christianity Today, August 12, 1996.

2   See the issue of color-blind approach to theology and bible and its impact on Asian American evangelicals in "Colorblind and Purpose: How differences can also bind" in ISAAC blog, www.isaacweb.org. In the blog, Tseng shares his powerful journey of overcoming color-blind theology and history, and its impact on Asian American evangelical Christians in particular.

we still suffer from the void of Asian American theological constructions and the lack of representation of our narratives in seminary curriculum. Consequently, seminarians suffer from this dismissal of theological and cultural identity.

THE IDEA IS BORN

While teaching at Fuller in the early 1990s, I became aware of numerous requests from local Asian American church pastors for bilingual pastors to serve the youth and young adult population. Today, Asian American churches still confront a leadership shortage exacerbated by the silent exodus. For this reason, in 2008, ISAAC initiated dialogs with Dean Howard Loewen at Fuller Theological Seminar and the idea for an inaugural Asian American Equipping Symposium was born.

As fellow African American pastors would say, "When you don't have teeth to chew, gum it," and in implementing our vision, we began relying on daily divine whispers and riding along the whimsical wind of the Spirit. After the initial conversations with Dean Loewen, a partnership emerged with the Office of Alumni and Church Relations under the leadership of Associate Vice President Mary Hubbard Given. Simultaneously, Given and I talked about a pilot gathering with Fuller's president and Asian American pastors. On June 16, 2009, I and a group including local Asian American pastors had breakfast with Fuller's President, Richard J. Mouw, during which he proposed key ecclesial questions that all seminaries need to pursue:

1. What is God doing in the world?
2. What ought the church be like to align with what God is doing in the world?
3. What ought the seminary be like to align with what God is doing in the world?

He challenged, " ... our focus needs to be on what God is doing and how Asian American churches can align with that rather than on issues that will sustain and grow the churches for their own sake."[3]

In this setting, lively discussions explored the question, "Having gone through theological education in a seminary and then having been in ministry more than

---

3 The entire minutes on "Living Out The Gospel: Asian American Contributions and Challenges" from the first Asian American Pastor's Breakfast, co-sponsored by ISAAC-SoCal and Fuller Theological Seminary on June 17, 2008 is available on ISAAC website, www.isaacweb.org.

ten years, what do you wish that you would have learned here?" Kevin Doi, a third generation Japanese American, pastor and founder of Epic Church in Fullerton shared,

> It feels good just to be included and heard because we have been neglected and ignored until now. I think that it is important that we embrace our identities as Asian Americans and also engage with the larger culture. To do so, we need to have a voice from our context.

James Yu,[4] a Chinese American pastor raised pertinent questions,

> But if we don't' know our identity, how can we give it up? Do we need to give it up at all to be a neighbor? Also, is it more that we can't articulate or that we don't have the permission to articulate who we are? This issue touches upon an important theological issue. If God is bringing together people from all tribes and tongues, how can we bring in the uniqueness of these communities without assimilation into an American society?

In response to Yu, Wing Pang stated,

> I said thirty years ago what James is saying now. Unfortunately, it still hasn't been heard ... It seems that many seminarians want to know about the Bible and the culture; they think that they already know the Asian American context. However they realize after pasturing a few years that they never knew the Asian American context.

Doi's questions hit the mark:

> Seminary wasn't very helpful in equipping me to discern the culture of my church. Discerning my church's culture is important for everything. How do we tell our stories? How do we communicate? We have to discern culture because culture is there. We might not be aware of it, but others are aware of it when they come in our midst. In a way, self-awareness as a com-

---

[4] James Yu pastured in Irvine as a youth pastor and is appointed as Vice President of Advancement at Logos Evangelical Seminary, El Monte, California as of April 2010.

munity is what is required.

In contrast, Jin Bae, a Korean American pastor shared his counter-experience. He believed himself to be contextualizing when subscribing to Rolling Stone magazine or watching MTV to engage the larger youth culture, only to discover that his Korean American youth were not interested in such media. Rather, they placed higher value on the Bible. Bae also noted that the *hurt and pain* felt among Korean American youth were quite different from those of white youth. As a result, Bae said, "It became difficult for me to learn how to contextualize on my own."

This first Asian American pastors' breakfast with President Mouw paved the way for the inaugural Asian American Equipping Symposium in November 2-3, 2009. May I extend special thanks to the ISAAC-Southern California Advisory Council members who met numerous times and offered their timely input throughout: Bill Watanabe, Wing Ning Pang, Shana Won, and Esther Lee. Our intern, Tracy Lee, graciously offered her God-given talents in graphic design. At the Symposium itself, Mary Hubbard Given (Fuller's Associate Vice President of Alumni/ae and Church Relations) and her office staff, Bert Jacklitch and Bonnie Stevens provided invaluable help. The efforts, support and wise council of all these friends and others helped make possible this journey of faith.

AAES PROGRAM HIGHLIGHTS

The keynote speaker, Dr. Jonathan Tran, Assistant Professor of Christian Ethics at Baylor University, framed his lectures on the past and the future of Asian American churches with a "both-and" paradigm, not an "either-or" paradigm. It was the right approach in light of the multi-faceted theme of "bridging" at the Symposium. Bridging theologies within the Asian American churches, the past with the future, and diverse intra-Asian American ethnic groups, Tran walked us through the interpretive path that was so rich in its content and candid in delivery. Tran captivated participants with vivid biblical narratives that resonated with Asian American journeys. The panel responses on Monday included three Fuller faculty members and Asian American pastors: Jehu J. Hanciles, Mark Lau Branson, Miyoung Yoon Hammer, Charlene Jin-Lee, Kenneth Fong, Benjamin Shin, Michael Lee, and Charles Lee.

Bishop Stephen Leung shared words of encouragement and benediction. Depicting the father of the prodigal son, running toward his son, Bishop Leung admitted, that he too does not run toward his son but waits for his son to show up to him.

On Tuesday, Tran addressed why Asian American Churches are the Future. The panelists included Charlene Jin Lee, Timothy Tseng, Charles Lee, and Benjamin Shin. Gender issues in Asian American churches in particular, discussed by Charlene Jin Lee, captivated everyone. Tran continued dialogue by email exchanges with Jin Lee even after his return to Texas. The luncheon speaker, Tommy Dyo, a Fuller alumnus from the 1990s, sketched a history of Asian American students at Fuller.

The breakout sessions, under the guidance and leadership of Jonathan Wu and Melanie Mar Chow, participants were divided into four topics for discussion and strategic thinking:

1. The future of Asian American pastoral leadership
2. The future of Asian American women in ministry
3. The future of the intergenerational Asian American church
4. The future of theological formation in Asian American churches

We are grateful to all who participated in such constructive conversations and substantive outcomes. We deeply appreciate participants' clear recommendations to keep traction and momentum going forward.

One necessity for such traction and momentum is *documentation*. This issue of the SANACS journal is an ideal setting for just such documentation. May these papers help the November 2009 Asian American Equipping Symposium continue to bear good fruit for both the academy and the church.

KEYNOTE PRESENTATION #1

Why Asian American Christianity has No Future:
The Over Against, Leaving Behind, and Separation From of Asian American Christian Identity

BY **JONATHAN TRAN**
BAYLOR UNIVERSITY

INTRODUCTION

The social theorist Naomi Klein speaks of "an impulse to dream" and the need for us to "think our way out of the present."[1] We live in a world of crushing homogeneity that wants to make us all the same. In the context, we have become impoverished dreamers. In a world of overwhelming suffering, violence, and sadness, our dreams have become small, our impulses diminished, thinking beyond the present unlikely. I offer my two presentations as attempts at dreaming, as a way to think our way out of the present.

I want to talk about the single most important issue I believe is facing the Asian American church, and that is its future. It is certainly a goofy academic thing to say that the future is the greatest challenge to any community, for of course, the future of a community is always its greatest challenge. But when I say the future is the greatest issue facing the Asian American church, I don't mean simply what will happen to it, will it survive, how will it grow, so on and so forth. Of course these are questions that demand the attention of our pastoral and seminary leaders. But by "future" I mean something more specific.

When I say the future is *the* issue facing the Asian American church I mean that because of its current identity, constitution, its historical development and its likely trajectory, I wonder *how* it is that the Asian American church will survive into the future, or *whether or not* it will survive, or whether that which survives will *continue* to be faithful to its unique calling.

What makes me worry that the Asian American church has no future? *Is it*

---

1 Klein makes these comments in the documentary, "The Possibility of Hope," written, directed, and produced by Alfonso Cuarón and embedded in the 2006 Universal Pictures DVD *Children of Men*.

because the church isn't coming up with innovative new ministries? Is it because it isn't developing a new core of leaders and a new vision? *Is it* because it hasn't renovated its buildings, or updated its technology, or changed out its worship styles to fit the newly emergent context of late modern capitalism, that it hasn't kept pace with the internet revolution and globalization? Do I worry that the Asian American church is not concerned with the future *enough*, and therefore does not have a future?

No, my fear is not that the Asian American church has *no* concern for the future, but rather that its interests are so focused on the future that it has little concern for the past. It simply lacks a past sufficient for its survival. In recent years, as the Asian American church has emerged from the Asian church in America,[2] it has become so enamored with a certain kind of future, a certain kind of survival, so interested in innovation and new things (new worship, new buildings, new pews, new styles) that it has relinquished the best parts of itself in order to purchase a future that will prove incommensurate to its calling. It has traded in its past, its history, its constitution as a tradition, and in doing so has left behind the resources it, like any moral tradition, needs to survive faithfully into the future.

More importantly, the problem with leaving behind your past is that the past is the only record Christians have that God will be faithful to them in the future. The Bible is the church's living memory of God's faithfulness; only by attuning our lives to it, do we know what the future holds, what kinds of futures are good for us, and that we have a future at all (Jos. 1). For Christians, the past is not just the past, but the always present promise that God remains with us.[3]

---

2   I request the reader's patience regarding a distinction I use throughout this paper, between Asians and Asian Americans. By Asian, I mean first generation immigrants from Asia; by Asian American, I mean the children of Asians, and hence second, third, fourth, etc. generation Asian Americans. This is a crude distinction to be sure, for no less reason than the suggestion that a recent immigrant isn't American and hence the concomitant implication that America is not entirely constituted by immigrants. Of course first generation Asians are just as "American" as ninth generation Asian Americans. I simply use the heuristic of "Asian" and "Asian American" throughout in order to name what I perceive to be the cultural distinctions between generations. As I characterize at different points, these distinctions come by way of language, cultural habits, socialization, so on and so forth. Most specifically, I make a distinction, that I believe while crude is temporarily helpful, between "Asian churches" and "Asian American churches" and here I deploy my "Asian" and "Asian American" distinction for the sake of describing different modes of Christian and ecclesial life.

3   It is through the past that we see God in the future. It is by remembering the scriptural claim of God's word to the Hebrews, "Of all the peoples of the Earth, I have called you Israel to be my people" that the Gentile church can be certain that this same God who has now called them will be faithful, in the words of St. Paul, to bring you to completion in the day of Christ Jesus our Lord (1 Thes. 5). It is in the past that we see God being faithful to the Jews even in their darkest hours. And it was by remembering that past that the earliest Christians remembered that God too would

The noted political theorist Hannah Arendt believed that any moral community exists at each moment between past and future. It is in this instance, in this fragile and always vanishing moment between past and future, that a community determines itself *from* the past *for* the future. According to Arendt, the past bestows a community the resources to know how to negotiate the unknowable future, to chart a course when the present is always vanishing. It is by the past that one generation passes on to the next generation a viable future for its children. Without the past, no community can know how to go on.

As a Jew and a German migrant to America during the Nazi era, Arendt could speak with some authority about what it means to survive. As a Jew she understood well that the past, and the past's many testaments to God, provided a community the courage to imagine a future even in the darkest present. As a German she knew that without a strong anchoring in the past, the future will not only breed monstrosities, but perhaps more deadly, a community will lack the resources to know how to fend off those monsters. And as an American, Arendt was keenly aware that the new is always only as good as the past from which it comes.[4]

So what do I mean when I say that the Asian American church lacks a past, and therefore also a future? Simply, to the extent that the Asian American church identifies itself as an over-against, a leaving behind, and a separation from. From what is the Asian American church over against, leaving behind, and separating? First, Asian American Christianity sits racially *over against* non-Asian American Christians; without its brothers and sisters, it loses its past as a common faith. Second, Asian American Christianity grew up by *leaving behind* its first generation forebears; without its immigrant mother churches, it abandons its past as a common story. Third, Asian American Christianity *separates itself from* the theo-

---

be faithful to them in their impending dark hours. I suppose that God could have chosen some other means by which to remind us of his faithfulness, could have chosen something other than time by which to bless our lives in time, but as God created us timeful creatures, so it is through and in time that the God of time has come to us. God has made it that the past serves as the lens through which we see God in the present and in the future. We understand from our medieval theological fathers and mothers that God is timeless and unbound by time, but we also know from the tradition that though God has no time in him, he, out of love for us his timeful creatures is eternally present to time through the incarnation of the Word and the ongoing presence of the Holy Spirit. For the Christian church, there can be no future if there is no past. See, for example, Thomas Aquinas, *Summa Theologica* (Allen: Thomas More Publishing, 1981), I1.10.2, Ia.9.1. Karl Barth, *Church Dogmatics II.1: The Doctrine of God* (London & New York: T & T Clark, 1957), 82-83.

4 Hannah Arendt, *Between Past and Future: Eight Exercises in Political Thought* (New York: Penguin, 1993), 3-40. On the question of difference and assimilation, see Arendt's elaboration of "the pariah" and "the parvenu" in *Rahel Varnhagen: The Life of a Jewish Woman*, trans. Richard and Clara Winston (New York: Harcourt Brace Jovanovich, 1973) and also her *The Origins of Totalitarianism*, 56-68.

logical tradition; without theology, it surrenders its past as a common language. It's this triple departure that worries me. Without the past, we Asian American Christians are headed into a future of our own choosing; having left so much behind, we lack going on well. Let me explain what I mean by 1) An Over Against, 2) A Leaving behind, and 3) A Separation from.

AN OVER AGAINST

To be American is to be racialized.[5] To come to America then is to enter into the peculiarly American experience of racialization, to be understood as a *Race* American: *African* American, *Mexican* American, *Asian* American. In coming to America, in becoming racialized, one gains an identity inscribed by these racial dynamics as the *ultima ratio* (ultimate rationale) of civic life. This is what the Ugandan Priest and theologian Emmanuel Katongole means when he says, "I didn't know I was Black until I came to America."[6] To be American is to think like a Race American.

In Race America, especially under the auspices of multiculturalism, to be racialized is to be separated into your own group *over against* other groups.[7] In

---

5 It has been known for sometime now that race rather than being factual is constructed. In other words, race is no thing. Rather, race is a culturally scripted performance; the so-called factuality of race can only be held — we only believe in the reality of race — to the extent that its mythical articulations get enacted over and over again. Here we see race, and what Kenan Malik calls "the discourse of race," in clear Nietzschean terms, where the "truth of race," and its primary designations (black, white, yellow, etc), is but a "mobile army of metaphors." Friedrich Nietzsche, "On Truth and Lie in the Extra-Moral Sense" www.geocities.com/thenietzschechannel/tls.htm; Kenan Malik, *The Meaning of Race: Race, History and Culture in Western Society* (New York: New York University Press, 1996). On the constructed nature of identity, see Michel Foucault's comments in "Neitzsche, Geneology, History" in *language, counter-memory, practice: selected essays and interviews*, ed. Donald F. Bouchard, trans. Donald F. Bouchard, 139-164 (Ithaca: Cornell University Press, 1977); Foucault's reflections on race in *The History of Sexuality: Volume I An Introduction*, trans. Robert Hurley (New York: Vintage, 1990), 145-150; Judith Butler, *Gender Trouble: Feminism and the Subersion of Identity* (New York: Routledge, 1999); and J. Kameron Carter, *Race: A Theological Account* (Oxford: Oxford University Press, 2008).

6 Emmanuel Katongole, "Greeting: Beyond Racial Reconciliation," in *The Blackwell Companion to Christian Ethics*, eds. Stanley Hauerwas and Samuel Wells 68-81 (Oxford: Blackwell Publishing, 2004), 68-69.

7 Any discourse no matter how contingent is as real as its effects. In America the inscriptions of race are thick. We Americans, unlike other cultures, script our regular political, social, and interpersonal lives with layered, stubborn, even demanding notions of race. To be American, unlike other places in the world, is to be racialized. The political theorist David Theo Goldberg suggests that in a postmodern age, in an epoch where individualism and difference rule, the only thing that holds together any type of common life is race, that race has become the lowest common denominator of what keeps us together. David Theo Goldberg, *The Racial State* (Oxford: Blackwell, 2002). In other words, a community may not share anything else in common (political affiliation, religious tradition, occupation, even hobbies) but as long as it shares race, it shares a communal existence. For a theological interpretation of the corrupted politics of sameness, and hence difference and

these groupings, or ghettos, or subcultures, the only thing that substantially holds us together, the only reason we exist as a group, the only thing that makes us unique as a distinct racial community, is that we are not like the others. These groupings are less about what we share in common than about what we don't share with others. In other words, these various racial groupings have less to do with *what you are* than *what you are not*. As a Race American, you know for certain one thing, you are not another kind of Race American. As an Asian American, you know you are not an African American, a white American, or a Mexican American. Now you would be very hard pressed to say what it is that makes you Asian American, but you know for certain, you are not black, Mexican, or white. Now you may know you are of Chinese descent or that you prefer Korean rice over Vietnamese rice, but none of this is to be Asian American; to be Asian in America is simply to not be something else.[8]

So if to be a Race American is to be over against, then what is "Asian American" over against? Most directly, we are over against Asians. We are ethnically Asian but culturally Asian American and hence define ourselves over against the experiences, histories, cultures, practices, and languages of first generation Asian people. While we are the children of immigrants, we ourselves did not go through the process of immigration. Though we may speak Asian languages, we do not conceptualize the world through those linguistic habits. While we look Asian, we are not Asian in the same way *those* Asians are Asian. You know the over against posture of Asian Americans by the embarrassment we often feel regarding those who are Asian by way of accent, dress, mannerisms, language, habits, etc. The whole lexicon of the "F.O.B." nomenclature signals this. While I, an Asian American, was born here, you are "fresh off the boat" which explains why you have the accent, dress, mannerisms, language, and habits and I don't.

But in the same way that Asian Americans are not Asians, we are also not American, at least according to other Americans. Unlike other Americans, we are removed from immigration (and hence Asian nationality) by only one or two short generations. Unlike other Americans, we do not as legitimately belong here. America is not our home, so the argument goes, in the same way that America is

---

descrimination, see William T. Cavanaugh, "The City: Beyond Secular Parodies," in John Milbank, Catherine Pickstock and Graham Ward, eds., *Radical Orthodoxy* (New York: Routledge, 1999).

8 These dynamics help explain the difficulties of inter-racial existence, those who possess multiple races, the so-called mulatto. If one knows whom she by knowing who she is not, then what happens when one is and is not simultaneously. These questions are explored in Brian Bantum's important forthcoming book *Mulatto Theology: Identity, Discipleship, and the Birth of a New People* (Waco: Baylor University Press, 2010).

home for the Irish-American. And we are continuously reminded of this. For example, someone may ask us, as they often ask me in the South, "Son, where are you from?" If I say, "California," they say ... (Wait for audience to fill in the blank), that's right, "No, where are you *really* from?" by which they mean from where did I emigrate. A few years ago, when American Olympian Michelle Kwan was defeated by fellow American ice skater Tara Lipinski, the headlines of one reputable newspaper read, "American beats Kwan." To the extent that "American" looks something like a person of Nordic facial features, then Asians, by physical features, will always be considered outsiders, no matter how many generations we've lived in America. So for Asian Americans, no matter how much we want to be "full fledged Americans", the racial politics of America don't often allow it. So we are on the one side, over against first generation immigrant Asians, and on the other side, we are over against non-Asian Americans. This dual over against doubly binds us on both sides, framing us into necessarily defining our identity not in terms of what we are, but what we are not.

Asian Americans know they are Asian Americans because they are not white and, they are certainly, in their minds, not black. They are over against whites specifically because while they would like to be white, they cannot be. As well, they are over against blacks specifically because they don't ever want to be black. They want to be white not in the sense of what they consider a cultural blandness but because they too want to live in certain neighborhoods, and have access to certain kinds of jobs and exercise certain kinds of power. As well, they don't want to be black because they fear what the African American has become in America, the pariah, the paragon of what one should not be in becoming racialized; in the same way they want to be white because of what whites have, they fear blacks because of what they *do not* have. While many Asian American youth may mimic a media perception of African Americans, very few Asian Americans would dare affiliate with the intense racial struggle endemic in black America.[9] We just want to rip them off whenever it's convenient for us. We're ultimately not sure what makes us any different from them, but for certain we know that they are not us. In this way, Asian American racialized life is but a microcosm of racialized life in America, where difference as a problem becomes the animating question of the civic nation. Hence, W.E.B. Dubois talked about a "double consciousness" that

---

9   See Patricia Hill Collins' *Black Sexual Politics: African Americans, Gender, and the New Racism* (New York: Routledge, 2005), 119-180.

meant he as a black man understood his very existence as that of a problem.[10]

In his magnificent history of immigration and what he calls the "alchemy of race" Yale historian Matthew Frye Jacobson describes the 20th century in terms of two simultaneous racial developments. Prior to the 20th century, there had been a ranking of Europeans such that whiteness, and its encodings for power and privilege, was reserved for Anglo-Saxons and denied to the likes of Eastern Europeans or Jews. However, in the 20th century there emerged what Jacobson calls, "multi-ethnic pan-whiteness" that now imagined "whiteness" as inclusive of even the likes of Eastern Europeans and Jews. This "pan-whiteness" did require as a prerequisite that those who desired to be white do two things: first, shed identity markers that were not white (for example, using whitening cosmetics to hide the skin color of Eastern Europeans, or discarding of ethnic Jewish practices and habits); second, perpetuate acts of discrimination against non-whites in order to prove they were white. In other words shedding ethnic identity and committing violence against non-whites purchased one's passage into whiteness.

This led to the second development. At the same moment that this multi-ethnic pan-whiteness came into existence, a new outsider was created: namely, those unable to shed ethnic identity or unwilling to do violence against blacks. The allowance of passage into whiteness simultaneously placed an albatross upon those unable to pass into whiteness. Violence and discrimination against those unable or unwilling to pass into whiteness was now justified on the grounds of that inability or unwillingness.[11]

I fear that Asian American churches as well are beginning to develop something like these realities. The development of multi-ethnic Pan Asian communities, similar to the development of the multi-ethnic pan-whites, most powerfully articulated in the Pan Asian American church, operates according to the same logic and involves the same kinds of political capital. Asian Americans prove they are Asian Americans over against Asians by shedding Asian markers, for example, by working as hard as possible to shed their accents. The goal here is to free ourselves of anything that marks us as distinctively ethnic persons. I think

---

10 W.E.B. DuBois, *The Souls of Black Folk* (New York: Vintage, 1990). Famously, DuBois writes, "Between me and the other world there is ever an unasked question: unasked by some through feelings of delicacy; by others through the difficulty of rightly framing it. All, nevertheless, flutter around it. They approach me in a half-hesitant sort of way, eye me curiously or compassionately, and then, instead of saying directly, How does it feel to be a problem?..." (ibid.).

11 Matthew Frye Jacobson, *Whiteness of a Different Color: European Immigrants and the Alchemy of Race* (Cambridge: Harvard University Press, 1998), 91-135.

here of one of my former students Yen Huong, a young Vietnamese American woman. Recently, Yen changed her first name to Kimberly, because "Yen", she was told over and over again, was hard to pronounce. So now she is Kimberly Huong. Well, Yen, now Kimberly, was also recently engaged, and her fiancé's last name is Dill, and so to her lament she realizes that within a few short years, she will have gone from Yen Huong, a name that is obviously Vietnamese, to Kimberly Dill, a name shorn of any ethnically Asian markers whatsoever.[12] Within Jacobson's continuum, that's the first move.

The second move is then to perpetrate violence over against. Hence Asian Americans prove they are Asian Americans by making fun of Asians who cannot but speak with accents.[13] For lots of second and third generation Asian Americans, making fun of and mocking first generation Asian immigrants (very often their parents) become a rite of passage of leaving behind Asian-ness and becoming Asian American. I *validate* my membership within Asian America by doing violence to *non*-Asian Americans, which include whites, blacks, Mexicans, etc.[14] Let me offer an example. It has become common for Asian Americans to make money by establishing businesses that glean off the surface of the urban poor, using their desperation for profit, while rarely if ever investing in their local economies or building up their local infrastructures; we make money *off* them, but we refuse to befriend them; we build our wig shops and liquor stores *there* but our houses and churches *elsewhere*.

Jacobson's double move of shedding ethnic markers and doing violence is most tragically demonstrated by the forms of violence Asian Americans perpetrate against themselves, against their own bodies in the great pursuit of western

---

12   Of course, "Kimberly Dill" is as ethnic as "Yen Huong" but since we live under the illusion that whiteness is ethnic-free, we don't think of ethnicity when we think of "Kimberly Dill, just as we assume "Yen Huong" is necessarily more difficult to pronounce than "Kimberly Dill," whereas for many people, "Yen Huong" is just as easy, or easier, than "Kimberly Dill."

13   For a humorous but sad depiction of the lengths traveled in order to shed accents, see Karl Elliott's *Better than Well: American Medicine Meets the American Dream* (New York: W. W. Norton & Co., 2003), 5-27.

14   No doubt some of this over against I have been discussing is in direct response to the ways in which Asian Americans have themselves been the victims of racial violence, discrimination, and segregation. As a person who grew up and currently lives in areas where Asians are the absolutely minority, I understand this. Regardless, an over against mentality will ultimately prove only to be a furthering of cycles of violence, discrimination, and segregation. Asian Americans are uniquely positioned, being both victims and perpetrators, of ending, rather than continuing cycles of racism.

conceptions of beauty and sexuality.[15] In what has now become standard practices for Asian American women, plastic surgery that sharpens the broad nose, increases the flat chest, or "Americanizes" the Korean eyelids, use the brutal violence of cosmetic surgery to, combining Jacobson's two moves into one, remove Asian markers by committing violence against Asian identity. Today, plastic surgery has become for Asians what the skin-lightening cosmetic industry was for Eastern Europeans a century ago. If race is only substantiated, if it is made real, by its performances, these are the performances by which Asian Americans become a race.

The Asian American church at its best moments is Christian.[16] The rest of the time, Asian American Christians import their racial idols into their churches, as if

---

15 No text illustrates this with greater insight and clarity than Toni Morrison's heartbreaking *The Bluest Eye* (New York: Vintage, 2007).

16 In those moments, it celebrates the one Trinitarian God, who while different persons — Father, Son, and Holy Spirit — is one essence and determined by one will and one love. Created in this image, Asian Americans reflect this image. At its best, the Asian American church inculcates its congregants into the story of God's people Israel, and God's covenant of promise into which the Gentiles are engrafted, and only by which are they saved. At its best, the Asian American church tries to approximate the prolyptic gathering of the nations, first promised in Genesis, commissioned in Acts and fulfilled in Revelation (Genesis 2; Genesis 10; Acts 2; Acts 10). There, in manifold worship together stand every people, nation and tongue from all peoples, all nations and all tongues (Rev 5).

At its best, the Asian American church is just one among many gathered around the one gathered body of Christ; we are many parts, but one body; we drink the same cup and eat the same bread. "For Christ is our peace; in his flesh he has made all groups into one and has broken down the dividing wall, that is, the over against between us ... that he might create in himself one new humanity in place of the two, thus making peace, and might reconcile both groups to God in one body through the cross, thus putting to death that over against ... " (Ephesians 2:14-16), if I can be permitted to restate scripture. At its best, the Asian American church, like the church universal, proclaims in one voice: difference is no problem for us; rather difference is a reflection of the Trinitarian life in which we participate. Difference is no problem for us because we happen to worship the One who in his own person hypostatically gathered the divine and the human, the creator and the created, divinity and humanity so as to reconcile us all to God. And so difference is no problem for us because it is no problem for God and it is no problem for God because God himself is no over against but a both/and: both three and one, both human and divine, both difference and identity. We the gathered of God, in our best moments, in our various cultural and linguistic expressions, testify to this gathering of difference, a sharing rather than an over against.

Without a corporate identity of the church as the church, without a vision of reconciliation gathered around the one gathered body of Christ as fully God and fully man, then we are each left to our own devices. This over against will leave us each thinking that we are now left to fend for ourselves, that we are not part of something bigger, which in consequence only inflates our sense of our own bigness in our own individual big heads. All of a sudden rather than understanding ourselves as participant in God's on-going covenant of promise as extended from the Jews to the nations, rather than a sense of shared history as a shared storied, we understand ourselves as the church alone. We don't seek to learn and partner with others because we keep forgetting there are others. We don't commingle with others because we have learned to understand our identity not as a mutual gathering but an over against. Over against Asians, with whom we share a past through our histories of immigration, over against other non-Asian American Christians, with whom we share a past because of the commonweal of Christianity. Hungry for identity and place we leave the one identity and place that might give us a chance. We leave the past and hence give up the future.

their Christianity had nothing to say to their Asian American-ness. In this way, the racial habits of Asian American *Christians* very often look no different than the racial habits of *non-Christian* Asian Americans. When this happens we abdicate the message of reconciliation to the violence of Jim Crow. Because we have not shown the world that the church is any better than a series of separate ecclesial water fountains, the world has set up its separate but equal water fountains.[17] Because we are an over against community, the only thing gathered in our churches is us, not them, and certainly not them. Rather than giving *away* the gospel, we have just *given* away the gospel. As Augustine says, the violence of the world is our fault, for the world knows nothing better.[18]

The specific problem with this over against mentality is that it segregates Asian American Christians from the universal church. The universal church shares a common past: we the nations have been called into God's covenant of promise. It is not because we are White, or Asian or Asian Americans that we warrant God's grace. It is only because God has baptized us into Jesus' Jewish body that we have been engrafted into a common history all nations now share with Israel. It is, as it were, by faith, and faith as a gift of God.

Without this common past, there can be no future. Any community that defines itself in terms of itself as an over against, as all Race Americans have been forced to do, has no future. Two things will happen, as these two things historically always happen. One, the lack of any constituent reason for being together other than being over against will produce a lack of resources necessary to negotiate our difference in relation to others' difference; we will turn increasingly internal, becoming so self interested as to implode upon the decadence of our racial singularity. Or, secondly, we will do what other racialized communities unable to negotiate their difference do; we will turn white, lacking any constituent identity we will long for the only identity that matters in America, the one identity

---

17 Race in America is one drinking fountain for blacks, one for whites, one for Latinos, one for Asians, so on and so forth. Mind you we are all drinking the same water, and the water does the same thing for our bodies, but either way, for each race, their own drinking fountain. Asian American Christians have swallowed race as such hook, line, and sinker. To be sure, Asian Americans have not done so any more than, for example, our Latino/a brothers and sisters. It does mean, however, that having accepted racialization without even a wee bit of resistance, we have become constant perpetrators of racial violence and discrimination over against our own Christian brothers and sisters. The separations that group the various racial communities in America are policed by way of violence, keeping some in by keeping others out.

18 At least this is John Milbank's reading of Augustine. John Milbank, *Theology and Social Theory: Beyond Secular Reason* (Oxford: Blackwell, 1993). Milbank understands this book as a inverted telling of Augustine's *City of God*.

that holds the cards of power and money and privilege and we will shed all the particularities that make us Asian: our languages, our foods, our celebrations, even our very names. We will sacrifice our color at the altar of whiteness. Either way, in this terrible but frighteningly near future, the Asian American church will, simultaneously, cease to be Asian American, and cease to be church.

A LEAVING BEHIND

Helen Lee's now classic *Christianity Today* article "The Silent Exodus" portrayed the slow series of events that has left many Asian churches in a lurch between generations — a curse, in some ways, of their successes of raising up subsequent generations of leaders in the rich soil of immigrant America.[19] In the same way that Lee's article in the 90s wondered whether first generation Asian ministries could effectively develop a second generation of Asian American leadership, so nearly fifteen years later, the question has become where these leaders have ended up. So well have these churches developed these young Christians that they soon outgrew their home congregations. The "Silent Exodus" names the story of how this next generation left their home churches in order to find greener pastures.

Let me offer an example. In one southern American city, a church grew out of a bible study started by Taiwanese immigrants who had come to America to study at a technical university. Feeling like second-class citizens in many of the predominately white churches in the city, they launched out, in search of something of their own. Over the years, the bible study grew into a church that became one of the largest Asian congregations in America. At its heyday the church could boast of a wonderful blend of young and older families, three generations of members, a thriving English Ministry alongside two thriving Chinese-speaking congregations, a multi-person pastoral staff team, and hundreds of committed Christians. Over the years, the children in this church grew into young adults. Again a product of the church's many successes, these young adults would go far away for university to schools like Stanford, Harvard, Carnegie Mellon, the University of Illinois, each an indication of how well these kids had integrated themselves into American society and the kinds of material wealth that church

---

19 Helen Lee, "Silent Exodus: Can the East Asian church in America reverse the flight of its next generation?" in *Christianity Today*, Vol. 40, No. 12 (August 12, 1996). Reprinted in *Asian American Christianity Reader*, ed. Viji Nakka-Cammauf and Timothy Tseng, 99-105 (Castro Valley: Pacific Asian American & Canadian Christian Education Project and The Institute for the Study of Asian American Christianity, 2009).

had come to expect. More importantly through the first generation's faithfulness in developing dynamic English speaking ministries the church produced powerful young visionary leaders, who in college found natural homes in groups like InterVarsity, Campus Crusade, and the like.

Though larger than most, this particular church epitomized hundreds of similar Korean, Chinese, Japanese, Filipino, Indian, or Vietnamese churches throughout the United States. Like many other immigrant Asian churches, the young adults that emerged from *this* church often spoke native languages, enjoyed Asian foods, and tended to hang out with similar looking people. But over time, variations between generations became increasingly evident. Though they spoke native languages, they clearly preferred to *express* themselves by *expressing* themselves in English, making it very unlikely they would pass on these languages to their own children. Though they enjoyed Asian food, their tastes both broadened toward pan-Asian cuisines and narrowed in their own ethnic foods i.e. no sea cucumber for this generation of Asian eaters. And though they hung out with other Asians, it was just as likely for them to marry Vietnamese if they were Chinese, Caucasian if they were Japanese or Korean, so on and so forth, again making it very unlikely that they would share any specific culture enough to pass it on to their own children. Finally, it wasn't simply their foods or dating tastes that were different, but their views and visions for what Christianity might be like, what discipleship demanded and promised, what studying the Bible meant; the basic sacramental lives of these Asian American Christians looked differently. In a sense, these variations always existed, but growing up highlighted these differences in especially pronounced ways. The successes of this Asian church meant its Asian American children took as seriously their faith as did their Asian parents; they, like the immigrant engineers that were their parents, sought something of their own.

Naturally, as the young adults in our southern Asian church grew up, preferred English, left behind sea cucumber, dated and married outside of their ethnic nationalities, and imagined Christianity differently than their parents, they began to feel less and less at home in what was once their home church. To them, the English ministry began to feel like an afterthought to the larger dominant Chinese congregation. Just as their parents had raised them, they refused to accept second-class citizenship in their own faith lives. So what happened? In what has become a paradigmatic description, Lee answers: "a silent exodus of church-raised young people who find their immigrant churches irrelevant, culturally stifling, and ill equipped to develop them spiritually ... " (99). These young adults left, often to find new church homes in culturally sensitive Caucasian churches, sometimes in pan-Asian versions of mega churches, and sometimes no church at all. Today, is there still an English-speaking Asian-American ministry in this predominantly first-generation Asian church? Yes, but most would be hard pressed to explain why, since the folks who attend that ministry feel like strangers to those in the other congregations, often not being able to even speak the same language, much less share in the same visions of Christianity. Indeed, the fastest growing group in this church is not the second generation Asian Americans, but rather the first-generation Indonesian community or the Mandarin speaking congregation.

This story of course can be told innumerable times with as many iterations as there are ethnic Asian churches. In response to the Silent Exodus, Lee foreshadows the development of pan-Asian churches like David Gibbons' Newsong and Ken Fong's Evergreen. These churches followed, and indirectly helped expedite, the Silent Exodus. Lee suggests, rightly I think, that these churches now epitomize the future trajectory of Asian American church life. Indeed, a few years ago, a conference Timothy Tseng and I attended featured "the future's top Asian American ministry leaders;" almost every future leader envisioned a church that looked something like Newsong or Evergreen, even against the warnings of Dave Gibbons and Ken Fong that theirs were specific instances of God's activity, and not to be taken as molds for every Asian American ministry. Unsurprisingly their caveats were left unheeded because when your church experience looks like a silent exodus, you cannot help but want to emulate the likes of Evergreen and Newsong. Not *one* future leader I spoke to hoped to join any of the mainline protestant denominations; none described liturgically-shaped and tradition-rich visions of worship; few expressed much hope for reconciliation and growth within their first-generation mother churches. A startling small number could articulate a coherent vision for a multi-ethnic church that was not determined by an over against approach to non-Asians. All these churches wanted to leave behind and start anew.

I would bet, though I'd be happy to be proven wrong, that in the years since this conference, almost 10 years ago now, the most thriving Asian American churches and congregations have indeed followed suit. *And* I am guessing these churches have found success because in the same way these future leaders wanted something like Evergreen, so the exiles of the Silent Exodus set out to find something like Evergreen. It was natural for these churches to find success since they had positioned themselves in response to the felt needs of these exiles; as surely as those churches failed, these churches succeeded. So a Rousing Success has met the Silent Exodus.

Accordingly, my doubts about the Asian American church's future seems to have run ashore on the success of the Asian American church which seems actually to have quite a bright future, especially if we take the Newsong's and Evergreen's as the barometers of success. This is precisely what has happened in the southern city of the church I have been discussing. The demise of the English Ministry at this particular church mirrored a similar exodus in other Chinese, Korean and ethnically Asian immigrant churches in this city. As this exodus began taking place and as people began to take notice, concurrently or perhaps consequentially, Asian American churches sprang up, and within a short period of time at least three such churches were growing. Today, these churches have to varying degrees succeeded in recouping these exiles, bringing them home in new homes, just as they left their former homes.

But I would like to take a moment to reflect on this success. And here I should be clear that my critique is only partially a critique of Newsong and Evergreen, for whom I have tremendous respect, and to which I am greatly indebted. My critique is at least partially aimed in the direction of these churches for at least two reasons. First, because these specific churches have had arguably the greatest influence upon the development of the larger Asian American church. Second, because these churches *are* our future and because they do exemplify the trajectory of Asian American Christianity and as exemplary deserve our sustained attention and consideration. It is to honor *not* dishonor these churches that I offer critique, for it is an indication of how seriously I take these ministries and their leaders. Still, my critique is not aimed *only* at these churches because I take these churches themselves to be only emblematic of larger concerns confronting all Asian American Christians. In other words, the Newsong's and Evergreen's were *not* the causes of the Exodus but themselves casualties of it. I tell the story of this southern Asian church in order to offer an example of how these processes were already underway long before Newsong or Evergreen ever showed up. These churches, like many of us, are only doing their best and represent I believe the most hopeful responses we have to the many paradoxes that grip

Asian American Christianity.

My concerns follow what I suggested at the outset of this lecture: can Asian American churches do well considering what they've left behind? If they order their lives by first leaving behind their pasts, what gets lost in the transition? My sense is that these churches and this new generation of Asian American Christian leadership want exodus — to leave their first-generation Asian mother churches — *without* the many losses *of* exodus. And this cannot be, for the scriptures tell us that exodus is fraught with loss, tragedy, mourning, and the many casualties of forgetting (Genesis 12-50; Exodus 1-40; Deut. 31-34; 1 & 2 Samuel). I don't believe Helen Lee's article had, nor have *we*, taken full stock of these losses; nor have we adequately thought through their implications. Much of the Old Testament narrative is the on-going question of memory: How well will the second and third generations remember God's faithfulness to the first generation? If they do not remember, if they choose to forget and leave behind their pasts, it is doubtful they will possess the resources to survive into the future.

What Lee's article and the notion of the Silent Exodus didn't theorize, even as it anticipated these new models of ministry, is what gets lost in the process. And I want to argue that what is lost in the Silent Exodus, what the children of exile do not carry forth, is precisely the resources that might otherwise help these congregations know how to be faithful. The tragedy here is two-fold. On the one hand, like prodigal children, upon receiving their inheritance, they quickly left their homes in anticipation of greener pastures (Luke 15).[20] Countless shrinking

---

20 It might be suggested that the progression of Asian American Christianity both from and eventually out of the Asian immigrant church can be interpreted within Old Testament images, especially Abram's departure in Genesis 12. However, I would raise an important distinction. The Hebrews essentially came to be in Yahweh's calling Abram forth from his motherland to the Promised Land, such that his departure became the mode by which God's people the Jews came to existence. However, this is markedly different than the transition from Asian to Asian American Christianity, where both generations are Christian (the transition here is not from non-Christian to Christian but from Asian to Asian American). A more fitting analogy would be the generational developments throughout the rest of Genesis, from Abraham to Isaac to Jacob and then Joseph, a thread I pick up in the next lecture. However, again, a critical difference obtains in that subsequent generations come to be not by leaving the predecessor generation. Indeed, the drama revolves around the tensions of remaining together, most powerfully illustrated by Josephs' return from forced (not chosen) exile and his generosity and reception toward his father and brothers. Joseph was forced out and yet still sought and provided the conditions of reconciliation. If anything, the continuity of Abraham's lineage suggest Asian American Christians continue, not depart from, the legacy of Asian immigrant Christianity. In some ways, I suspect they always do, even within these various departures, but in such cases, a greater association with Joseph-like mourning and hope need to prescind within Asian American Christianity. It might also be suggested that to the extent that a "blessing" is given, then the departure of Asian Americans from Asian immigrant churches is not abandonment. I imagine this to be the case at some level, but I do wonder as to what such a blessing would look like and I doubt that such a blessing is often sought on the part of departing Asian Americans.

Asian churches across America testify to this. Rather than enjoin in the hard work of generational reconciliation, rather than lean into the boundless reservoirs of wisdom these first generation congregations possess, we second and third generation Asian Americans have traded in our unassuming, old-fashioned, behind the times, old-world but faithful Asian church for the boisterous, sexy, loud smash and grab churches of the next generation of Christianity. I will admit, our parents dress poorly; they often speak through thick incomprehensible accents; they lack the requisite sense of humor to understand why Adam Sandler is a funny guy. Having first generation Asian Christians around is not, in other words, effective church growth strategy. To be sure much of the blame can be laid at the feet of the first generation for their unwillingness to accommodate the Spirit's new work in the next generation. To the extent that the first generation failed to invest fully in its children, its children felt put out enough that they left.

But they could have stayed. They could have struggled the way the church has always struggled from one generation to the next. They could have imagined life not in the terms of America's rugged individualism but in the terms of the Kingdom, which demands and promises that in the last days, your young women will see visions and your old men will dream dreams, a prophesy itself passed from one generation to the next (Joel 2; Acts 2). That staying rather than leaving is possible is testified by the thousands of Asian American Christians who have decided to stay with, rather than leave behind, their first generation Asian churches, even though those churches are old-fashioned, behind the times, even though the leaders of those churches don't dress well, don't laugh at Adam Sandler, and very often do not accommodate the Spirit's work in the lives of their children. *Why* have they stayed? I have no idea, but to guess somehow they thought it was the right thing to do. Somehow they believed that while old Asian immigrant Christians were not effective church growth strategies, their lives did have something to say about the goodness of the Gospel.

And this gets to the second part of the double-tragedy. Not only were the mother churches left behind when the second and third generations left, what was also lost was the ability to see that loss. Without a home, one forfeits the horizon by which to judge the road ahead; homeless, you surrender the compass by which to direct your own path. Without a home, you have no alternative but to leave. When you give up the generation that produced you, you also give up the grounds by which you are able to see well, to morally understand what is happening, to pay heed to the realities around you. The reason it was so seemingly easy for the second and third generations to leave their homes was because they did not know what they were doing; for how could they, since in leaving, they left behind their ability to do so. Having literally left their past, they left also their ability to understand the future.

A SEPARATION FROM

One reason we have not taken stock of the losses of the Silent Exodus and their implications for the newly emerging Asian American church is that we feel neither the inclination to do so, nor do we have the resources to know how to take stock even if we wanted to. Instead of those resources, which I call theological, I see running through these emerging churches the discourse of what the philosopher Alasdair MacIntyre called the "the goods of efficiency," or put simply, the "how to" guides derived from the importation of business and entrepreneurial enterprises into ecclesial life.[21] Put simply, the operating model of many emerging Asian American churches is the operating model of business.[22]

This business approach relies on what MacIntyre calls "the goods of efficiency" and takes as its primary registers questions bestowed, inherited by, and I'd argue, imposed upon church life as gleaned from the business world i.e. the world of profit, property, and possessions. It's my observation that market capitalism is the primary ethos running the Asian American church. To be sure, Christianity has never been completely devoid of the kinds of practical concerns the market deals with on a regular basis. For example, in Acts 6 we see as one of the first official duties of the New Testament church the question of properly apportioning adequate resources for widows of martyrs who have died for the faith. The allocation of deacons for this purpose, then and now, is mutually within the province of church and business. However, I'd say there is a marked difference. In Stephen's day, the first church leader appointed to allocate the resources for the widows, the goods of efficiency were measured against the goods of faithfulness (appropriated from MacIntyre's "goods of excellence"). Prior to the onslaught of

---

21 Alasdair MacIntyre, *Whose Justice? Which Rationality?* (Notre Dame: University of Notre Dame Press, 1989). Regarding the dangers of efficiency, also see Gerrald P. McKenny, *To Relieve the Human Condition: Bioethics, Technology, and the Body* (Albany, NY: State University of New York, Press, 1997), 25-38.

22 You'll know this initially by observing the description I've used here, "operating model" and acknowledge how much this phrase has taken residence in many Asian American churches where "chief operations officer" or "executive pastor" are now familiar parts of the church's vocabulary.

capitalism, faithfulness measured effectiveness and something effective would be rejected if it were deemed unfaithful. Today, as the discourse of business has become our ruling paradigm, the goods of efficiency have *become* the goods of faithfulness, so that faithfulness today is almost exclusively measured by effectiveness.[23]

Within MacIntyre's argument, the church has only two options once it has surrendered the goods of faithfulness to the goods of efficiency: namely, the managerial and the therapeutic. The church becomes a manager of individual desires, optimizing individual lives in order to achieve their own determined ends, and offering therapies when these ends fail to provide the promised happiness. However, as manager and therapist, at no time is the church in a position to challenge, reorder, or reject the ends individuals so choose for themselves. Since the Asian American church understands itself as primarily a manager of individuals, its pastoral task is primarily to assist people in getting what they want, not, as Augustine would say, shape those wants.

I see this everywhere in Asian American Christian life, where the demands and promises of discipleship to the Lordship of Christ have given way to the priority of the self-serving, self-interested, and self-diminished self. This is not to say that the selves produced in these congregations don't do good things, such as homeless ministries and quiet times. It's more that goods such as homeless ministries and quiet times have been instrumentalized for the self's satisfaction. Of course none of this is unique to the Asian American church, but I would say that Asian American Christians who garner the highest per capita incomes in America through their almost maniacal fixations with higher education are especially vulnerable to conflating the Gospel with the false promises of the American Dream.[24] Especially with their difficult histories of immigration and assimilation, Asian Americans, I believe, have a hard time distinguishing discipleship from upward mobility. Their churches, in turn, cannot help but endorse and even encourage this mindset and so cannot help but see themselves as managers and therapists of this mobility.[25]

---

23 See the debate between faithfulness and effectiveness between ethicists John Howard Yoder and Paul Ramsey respectively in John Howard Yoder, *The Politics of Jesus: Vicit Agnus Noster* (Grand Rapids, MI: Eerdmans; Paternoster Press, 1994), 228-233; and Paul Ramsey, *Speak Up for Just War or Pacifism: A Critique of the United Methodist Bishop's Pastoral Letter "In Defense of Creation"* (University Park: The Pennsylvania State University Press, 1988), 117-123.

24 See http://www.usatoday.com/news/nation/2009-11-15-asians_N.htm?csp=DailyBriefing.

25 Alasdair Macintyre, *After Virtue: A Study in Moral Theory* (Notre Dame: University of Notre Dame

Here you see the colluding effects of the losses that accrue with the "leaving behind" and the "over against." Since the Asian American church has torn itself away from its first generation forebears and set itself over and against non-Asian American Christians, it has surrendered its sources of moral deliberation, its traditions of truthfulness, and memories of God's faithfulness; alone and isolated, it has only itself to adjudicate the future. When you have no past by which to make decisions and no other communities by which to interpret the world, then the unknown future determines how you should do things, and hence it will be solely for the sake of the future, namely for the sake of survival of the present into the future, that one has to make decisions.[26]

This is what happens when the church separates from theology. The incarnational nature of Christian ministry means that context matters. Part of the task of theology is to contextualize context, to situate any particular church in its particular context upon the larger context of God's providential care of history and conversely to contextualize God's providential care of history as what he is doing within any particular church; theology helps us see what we're doing by seeing what God is doing. Without theology, we have no idea what we are doing, what we have done, or what we should do.

I have been told in no uncertain terms that my particular questions as a Christian theologian are simply unhelpful to the current plight of the Asian American church, which requires, according to this opinion, practical not theoretical assistance. Of course I would disagree with the notion that theology is simply a theoretical affair. (Remember that the controversies over orthodoxy in patristic literature were arguments about practical concerns like salvation, worship, and church leadership.) Still the accusation about theory is the suggestion that theology is sequestered in ivory towers, that the only people for whom theology is important is theologians. In contrast, the argument goes, the Asian American church is busy dealing with real matters in the real world. The implication is also

---

Press, 1984), 23-35.

26 In contrast, MacIntyre thinks that moral discernment takes place in continuity with the past, in such a way to be coherent, intelligible, and contiguous with a tradition's on-going existence in time. One makes decisions as if one was involved in an on-going conversation, and at that table are treasures old and new, assuming, that is, they are not left behind. This does not mean, for MacIntyre, that nothing new ever happens, but only that the new happens continuous with developments from the past; that is how a tradition remains faithful to itself, by retaining a sense of integrity with the best of its history. Without that past, it is not simply that one will make poor decisions, but more deadly, one will make poor decisions without knowing one has made poor decisions. If the future is marked by the concerns of survival, anything becomes acceptable for the sake of survival. One will then separate from all other concerns, especially those considerations that undermine the calculus of efficiency and the formulas for success.

clear: it doesn't matter, for example, if you get the Trinity right or wrong in thinking through issues like "the flow" of worship or developing a really cool small group ministry.

Such arguments are legitimated, I am told, by the further claim that seminary is the worst place you could go if you want to learn to grow a church, with the obvious implication being that churches don't need theology to be churches and that the kind of theological training one gets from seminary only slows down effective church growth or gets in the way of the emerging church. Better to get an MBA than an MDiv; if you want to be a good pastor, learn counseling, not systematic theology. Like I said, managers and therapists. In response I'd like to say, "Get your Trinity wrong, and you always get your worship and small group ministry wrong; it's just that without theology, it will take you some time to figure that out."[27]

Theology is the time God has given the church to talk about God in order that the church would not be ruled by efficiency but worship. From the perspective of efficiency worship must look like a waste of time. From the perspective of theology, worship is what time is for, and only in the context of worship do we theologically understand how to efficiently order our lives, and hence our time, to worship God well. In terms of what we have already discussed, without theology, the Asian American church can't possibly know its racial over against is endangering the gospel. Since the irresistible and ineffable processes of socialization racialize all Americans, without theology, Asian American Christians have no way to recognize or resist its bio-political powers. Likewise, since leaving behind the first generation works, because it's effective, we have no idea what we are doing when we leave other than we know it works. We lack the theological lenses to see how deeply problematic it is; without theology, we lack the conversations that might offer more creative alternatives than leaving. Already positioned over against and leaving behind, separating ourselves from theology allows us to do little work at these critical intersections.[28]

---

27 All these disparagements about seminary and theological questions point to a deep and now tired suspicion on the part of Asian American Christians regarding theology. At some point I don't know what to think of this since I know Asian Americans love higher education. As well, I'm not quite sure if Asian American suspicions about academic theology are any different than the larger suspicion of theology resident in most Evangelicalism. Perhaps the Asian American allergy to academic theology is just another instance of Asian American Christianity mimicking white Christianity.

28 In contrast, while white Christianity is equally evangelical and equally hesitant about theology, still, inhabiting the white and European Christian tradition, it can't help but run into these sourc-

And in turn theology has very little interest in Asian Americans. Simply put, the current state of the Christian academy considers the Asian American church irrelevant. This is counterpoised to secular academic interest on the topic of Asian Americans, finding there a dynamic and fascinating ethnography of realities, which have vast implications, warranting serious academic research and investigation. The Christian academy, by which I mean seminaries and confessional graduate programs in religion, in contrast, has little to no interest in the topic of Asian American Christianity.

Because of a worn binary that has fixated American race relations to a black/white distinction, all else is rendered invisible, as if the only thing that matters is how white people relate to black people. On this binary, Asian American Christians have a choice between these two options. The binary of white/black Christianity of course is determined by the primacy of whiteness, which leaves black Christianity simply derivative of a prior and more essential white Christianity. It is no wonder that within this binary, Asian American churches have overwhelmingly, I'd even venture to say totally, chosen the white option. Academic theology has chosen to align itself with white Christianity — vis-à-vis European and Anglophone theology — and every once in a while, though always with the greatest wariness, black theology. There is simply no room when white theology hogs the show, leaving almost no space for anyone else except some marginalized version of black theology.[29] In tomorrow's talk I will suggest that the emergence onto

---

es. For white Christianity, Karl Barth may not be avoidable. In contrast, for Asian Americans the German theologian Karl Barth can't help but seem like an outsider. As well, to the extent that the black church follows in the footsteps of the great witness of African American Christianity and its equivalencies in the Black literary tradition and the likes of the Harlem Renaissance, it can't "leave behind" nor does it want to its amazing tradition of moral discourse and deliberation. Because it understands itself as continuous with this tradition, it looks to the tradition to guide its deliberations about everything from Trinity to church worship to making really fantastic small groups. The black church does this no matter how hard things get, which allows it, according to Jeffrey Stout, to continue to be the black church even within the barbarism of American racial injustice. Jeffery Stout, *Democracy and Tradition* (Princeton: Princeton University Press, 2004). Asian Americans have left their tradition behind, or as first and second generation immigrants, simply lack sufficient traditions in the first place. Whereas even if African Americans wanted to leave behind the tradition of black Christianity, the blood of Christianity would still flow in their veins. Such blood does not flow through the long generations of Asian people, and hence is not available to Asian American Christianity. (Recently D. H. Williams has demonstrated the early historical presence of Christianity on the Asian continent, with Nestorian communities in Chinas as early as the sixth century. See "Christianity as a Religion of the East: Evidence for the Church in China.") The natural reservoir of theology as a tradition is not available as organically to the Asian American church, and so whereas at least theoretically the resources of Trinitarian considerations vis-à-vis Karl Barth are available for white church deliberations about the flow of worship or vis-à-vis James Cone's reading of Barth for black deliberations about small group, no such natural conduits exist for Asian American Christianity. And so Asian Americans have very little interest in theology, since it is not part of their ethnic or cultural histories.

29 Because Asian Americans situate themselves over against Asian immigrants, then the valuable

this stage of a generative Asian American theology has the potential to open the doors and recast how this stage is set. For now, it's enough to say that from the perspective of the overwhelmingly white Christian academy, Asian American Christianity doesn't matter. Neither black nor white, both victims and victimizers of racism, not Asian and not fully American, Asian Americans are simply ignored. They are rendered invisible by the registers of contemporary theology.

The problem with the Christian academy not caring about Asian American churches is that such a lack of regard leaves those churches increasingly vulnerable to any discourse that will grant it attention. If the discourses that are interested in and interesting *to* Asian American churches is on the one hand increasingly secular racial politics and on the other unapologetically parasitic business practices then the Christian academy strands the Asian American church to its death. This state of affairs is deeply problematic on ethical grounds if we remember that Asian Americans are increasingly filling the seats of America's best seminaries. From Princeton to Trinity Evangelical Divinity School to Fuller Theological Seminary, Asian Americans are paying lots of money — or borrowing lots of money — in order to be trained by the Christian academy. They pay for this education, imbibe the lessons of these teachers, master these materials, embrace this tradition, learn these languages all the while they're refused even an ounce of help in how to contextualize this education for the unique circumstances of Asian American Christianity.

The great 20th century theologian Karl Barth famously suggested the task of theology be undertaken with the Bible in one hand and a newspaper in the other. The world around us, Barth was asserting, really matters. And yet, seminary professors often teach and write as if the world doesn't matter, as if Princeton and the Korean American church don't share a common destiny through the Reformed tradition, as if thousands of Chinese American Christians don't look to TEDS for a coherent biblical hermeneutics, as if Fuller were not located in the most Asian place in the world outside of Asia. Talking about his experience at Fuller, one Korean American tells a story that characterizes the world around us:

> I was dating a Filipina for a while but was counseled by a Korean pastor that I could not have a non-Korean marriage because of my ministry. My

---

resources of liberation theology hold little value for them, because from the perspective of the Asian American, liberation theology speaks from, of and to an entirely foreign context.

Fuller professor told me that I should stay with my girlfriend. Perhaps that in the larger picture, this advice from the professor was right. However, I had no go-between as I heard two opposing views; I was in a context where two cultures were clashing. I needed a cultural translator. Fuller was a very formative time for me, as it is for a lot of people. In these crucial times, I wish that someone would have understood my context.

This is a regrettable state of affairs if only for the erroneous epistemological suggestion that truth can be truth without being incarnated. It is almost as if these institutions and these teachers only see white people when they see Asian American people. One Asian American woman stated, "I had no mentors at Fuller, which was a very hard thing for me to deal with. I wanted to challenge the assumptions of my culture with the gospel. Yet, no one could understand me at Fuller, so it was very difficult."[30]

Here we see a parallel to my earlier criticisms about businesses that take from the disenfranchised without investing in their infrastructures. If theology understands itself, as it has to in order to be faithful, as a servant of the church, it must divest its vast stores of goods for the benefit of its churches. If it does not, it will only have perpetuated a self-fulfilling prophesy by assuming the Asian American church politically irrelevant. This is happening to the great detriment of Asian American Christians desperate for help and to the great shame of academic theology, which will cease to be theology and simply be academic.

This lectureship and the recent efforts of President Mouw and the Fuller community are important steps in the right direction, as are professorships and centers in Asian American Christianity at places like PTS or American Baptist Seminary of the West. But still, we have a long way to go. What Asian American Christians so desperately need are courses for their contexts, *including* classes that dare to question their contexts, professors from and with interests in the Asian American church (hint, hint) — and the academy's encouragement that such scholarship count as "scholarly" — , classroom discussions that, as Pastor Wing Pang suggests, "theologize the Asian American context," academic centers that act as intersections between church and academy, bridging the academic and the

---

30 In contrast, consider the remarks of then Fuller professor Miroslav Volf in the opening pages of *Exclusion and Embrace: A Theological Exploration of Identity, Otherness, and Reconciliation* (Nashville: Abingdon Press, 1996), 13-16. Volf specifically names the contexts of riot torn Los Angeles, besieged Sarajevo, and the intellectual atmosphere of Potsdam. My sense is that traveling, which has marked Volf's career, forces greater awareness of context. Without traveling, context becomes less visible.

ministerial, and research projects and publications that help the whole church, not just its Asian Americans, think through these complex issues. In other words, what the Asian American Christian needs is what *every* Christian needs, and they need for others to see they need it. If not, Asian American doubts that seminaries and theologians have nothing worth considering will only continue. If not, the past, which is our theological inheritance, will be lost, leaving behind an ability to continue faithfully into the future.

CONCLUSION

Hopefully I have shown why the *over against* has no future, why the *leaving behind* has no future, why the *separation from* has no future, and why these dynamics bode ill for the future of the Asian American church. It is the collective consequences of these three departures from the past that worries me most. I fear that they are contributing to an interwoven deterioration of the basic constitution necessary for any Christian community to remain Christian. It is the combining of these three departures from the past that I see as slowly eroding our future, as slowing chipping away at the great gift that is the Asian American church.

KEYNOTE PRESENTATION #2
Why Asian American Christianity is the Future: Holding it Together in Yellow Christianity[1]

BY **JONATHAN TRAN**
BAYLOR UNIVERSITY

INTRODUCTION

In *Radical Hope: Ethics in the Face of Cultural Devastation*, Jonathan Lear examines a community staring down what the philosopher Martin Heidegger once called "the impossible possibility" of no longer being there.[2] Lear's wonderful little book depicts the Crow Native Americans at the most critical juncture in their long history: the brink of extinction. Having lived untold generations by common narratives, cultural practices, and linguistic habits, the Crow faced an unimaginable challenge with the arrival of the white man. It was not the white man's armies and modernized weapons, his disease or Christianity, or even his inexhaustible greed for land and seemingly natural propensities for wonton destruction that challenged the Crow way of being. No doubt the white man's modernized, Christianized violence had the potential to wipe the Crow Nation from the face of the earth. But then again, so had many other enemies. Indeed, it was this very ability to confront calamity and survive that engendered Crow existence. Danger was no threat to these people; in some ways, it was their very lifeblood. Rather, a far more encompassing menace loomed when the white

---

1   I realize that dubbing Asian Americans "Yellow" is hardly inclusive, for it does not capture the diversity of our Asian American brothers and sisters, which to be sure include many of those too often left out of "Yellow" or "Asian American": South Asians, Pacific Islanders, under-represented Asian minorities such as the Hmong, etc. Still, I also think that trying to include everyone is disingenuously ambitious, exactly to the extent that diversity by its nature slips the reigns of total inclusivity. I use "Yellow" in a purposefully limited way here, as a rhetorical device that seeks to narrate my experience with Americans of Japanese, Chinese, Taiwanese, Korean, and Vietnamese (and to a lesser degree Filipino/a and Cambodian) decent, discomfited to a politically valorized whiteness and blackness that currently dominates the methodological landscape. I could qualify ad nauseam "Yellow" to include others, but doing so would only exclude yet others while belying the obvious limits of my experience and scholarship as well as the narrow aims of this essay.

2   Jonathan Lear, *Radical Hope: Ethics in the Face of Cultural Devastation* (Cambridge: Harvard University Press, 2006). Martin Heidegger, *Being and Time*, trans. Joan Stambaugh (Albany: State University of New York Press, 1996), 238; and Martin Heidegger, *Introduction to Metaphysics*, trans. Gregory Fried and Richard Polt (New Haven: Yale University Press, 2000), 41.

men arrived and brought all that modernized and Christianized violence: the death of the buffalo.

If survival despite on-going danger constituted the fabric of Crow culture and if stories of past survival enabled them to imagine a future despite the most perilous challenges, then it was the buffalo that symbolized this life-battle between past and future. The buffalo were not simply a source of physical sustenance for the Crow, but indeed their cultural and spiritual emblem. Their entire way of life, their seasonal patterns, the basic trades of their people, their cultural routines, the trusted processes by which boys passed into manhood and women demonstrated their part in the vast and timeless community of Crow revolved around the buffalo. Take away the buffalo and you take away Crow existence. Hence it was a very specific violation on the part of white modernity and Christianity that led to the Crow Nation's cultural collapse.

Of course as the white men systematically and sometimes randomly slaughtered the buffalo, they had no idea they were visiting cosmic destruction upon a people; they knew not what they were doing, for how could they, themselves having traded their storied pasts for the adventures of the unknown future. So when the white men made a business of buffalo furs for pennies on the dollar or gamely shot buffalo for sport from shiny new intercontinental trains, they just thought it was fun; they had no idea they were destroying a way of life. But with each buffalo carcass, the Crow passed away. The Crow warrior chief Plenty Coup described what followed: "You saw what happened to us when the buffalo went away.... The hearts of my people fell to the ground, and they could not lift them up again. After this nothing happened. There was little singing anywhere." Plenty Coup describes, with great profundity, what happened to the Crow when he says, "After this nothing happened." There was no more future. The very thing that held past, present, and future together vanished, and as such, the Crow's long history ended; nothing *else* happened *any* longer.

Lear, a psychoanalyst deeply influenced by Heidegger's existential philosophy, is keenly interested in how people respond to a future without a future, how they tell the story of their lives when those stories no longer hold meaning.[3] He writes, " ... the problem goes deeper than competing

---

3   Lear draws on the work the Heidegger scholar John Haugeland, specifically "Truth and Finitude:

narratives. The issue is that the Crow have lost the concepts with which they would construct a narrative. This is *a real loss*, not just one that is described from a certain point of view. It is a real loss of a point of view." For the Crow, history had literally come to an end. Eventually, in Lear's telling of the story, the Crow Nation, though not their way of life, is saved when Plenty Coup receives a prophetic dream that enables him to imagine a future, to hold both present cultural devastation and the Crow's long past of survival together in a way that opens up a future for his people. Hence "radical hope" names for Lear a community's orientation "directed toward a future goodness that transcends the current ability to understand what it is" (32, 50).

Here I will try to imagine for Asian American Christians "a future goodness" that transcends our current abilities to understand what that future is. I think this is what lay leader Bill Watanabe means when he wonders about Evergreen San Gabriel, "What will it be like in ten years? Perhaps it will look like something that we are not familiar with at all." There are of course innumerable differences between Crow Native Americans and Asian American Christians, not least of which one is ending as the other is beginning, but they share at least one thing in common: finding themselves captive in what have become strange lands, they must find ways to hold it all together.

Here I will try to describe "a future goodness that transcends our current ability to understand it." For the Asian American church, what is this future goodness? In some way, since it transcends our current ability to understand, we don't know. This not knowing is life with the Spirit. Still, I would suggest that theology is one such voice that might help us discern this future goodness; theology might just be, like Plenty Coup for the Crow, a dream-like prophesy from the nowhere of the past that might give us a chance for the future. Most importantly, I want to suggest that the Asian American church is this future goodness, a future goodness that has yet to be understood. The Asian American church is a prophetic voice precisely in its betwixt and between pilgrim, migrant place in America. It is this future goodness that has the very real possibility of being *the* future goodness for not only Asian Americans but for all Christians and for all of America.

Heidegger's Transcendental Existentialism," in *Heidegger, Authenticity, and Modernity: Essays in Honor of Hubert L. Dreyfus, Volume 1*, eds. Mark Wrathall and Jeff Malpas (Cambridge: MIT Press, 2000). On Heidegger and death, see also Carol J. White's important *Time and Death: Heidegger's Analysis of Finitude*, ed. Mark Ralkowski (Aldershot: Ashgate, 2005).

HOLDING IT TOGETHER

The tragedy of the Asian American Christian over against, leaving behind, and separation from that I outlined yesterday is that it need not be this way. Though our community sits on a fault-line of tectonic contradictions (we are Asian American but not Asian; we are Asian American but not American; we are neither black nor white; we are the children of our parents, but we are not our parents; we are victims and we are victimizers; we are inheritors of a discursive tradition that sounds to us like a foreign language; so on and so forth), still, there is a way to hold it altogether. Or let me rephrase that: there *must be* a way to hold it altogether, for what other options have we? The impossible possibility of cultural devastation? Abdicating the many good graces that God created when God created Asian American Christianity? True, the dangers facing Asian American Christianity are formidable, but for us, no more formidable than the great calling that marks our lives as Christian: to be in but not of the world (John 17). Faithfulness to this is our great task, in a way that makes mere survival not nearly the triumph Lear asserts, who seems to think survival for the Crow people, rather than faithfulness to a way of life, is all that matters.[4] For Christians, survival is not our task, but faithfulness, even such that death — as the martyrs remind us — is sometimes our greatest faithfulness.

The future of the Asian American church is the future of the Christian church in America, and I would argue, the future of America. For in our future stands the fate of every community that struggles between the impossible possibility of cultural death and the equally impossible possibility of cultural faithfulness. In the future of Asian American Christianity sits the future of Christianity in this land, the ability to hold together the many complexes of our lives on the pilgrimage from the earthly city to the heavenly city. We must hold it together, because we have to. We *can* hold it together because the One who calls us to be in but not of the world was *himself* in but not of the world, and hence is able to bring to completion our great task.

This morning I juxtapose yesterday's over against, leaving behind, and separation from with holding together. Rather than over against, good moral traditions hold together the multiple allegiances that always constitute identity. In some sense, identity is nothing other than this holding together; especially within the

---

4 See Stanley Hauerwas' and Dave Toole's review in *The Christian Century*, Vol. 124, No. 23 (November, 2007).

context of late modernity, there are few identities that are not some amalgam between multiple traditions, narratives and visions of the good.[5] Rather than leaving behind, good traditions always hold together several generations at once as they journey between past and future; it is only the most deceived tradition that believes it has somehow transcended its past. Rather than separation from, good moral traditions lean into the past, learning from the vast stores of its discursive history in order to see rightly the challenges of the future; members of good traditions do not fear but indeed welcome past discourses as a conversation *about* them, a conversation that can't go on *without* them.

It is by tending the past that Asian American Christianity will find itself productive of the most amazing new possibilities. Returning to Hannah Arendt, it is precisely in the fragile moment between past and future that the generative processes of thought and action emerge onto the world-stage.[6] Rather than a future set over against a discarded past or one undercut by infinite repetition, the church exists in the Spirit-created sliver in between. In this holy space between what God has done and what God will do, the Asian American church gathers the fragments of its memories and through the courage of hope patches together a quilted future. It is *hard* work because it is *delicate* work, and the pieces that comprise our future are none other than the remainders of God's infinite presence that can never be contained and so surges forward, creating a future as the moreness of that presence. Those who dare minister in God's church require what the Psalmist calls "skillful hands and integrity of heart" because the past as living memory arrives as living flesh (Psalm 78:72). These cherished ones are indeed treasures hidden in earthen vessels and must be handled with care for they memorialize the Three-in-One God of eternity as also the past-present-future God of time (2 Cor. 4:7-18). Here the most innovative Asian American ministries flourish because they grow in the same rich soil where the Incarnate Word

---

5 In tandem with my comments on MacIntyre in the previous lecture, see Romand Coles' reading of MacIntyre in *Beyond Gated Politics: Reflections for the Possibility of Democracy* (Minneapolis: University of Minnesota Press, 2005), 80-108.

6 Consider Seyla Benhabib's interpretation, *The Reluctant Modernism of Hannah Arendt* (Oxford: Rowman & LIttlefield, 2003). Describing Arendt's work, Benhabib writes, "The task of this kind of political theory is to engage in 'exercises' of thought by digging under the rubble of history so as to recover those 'pearls' of past experience, with their sedimented and hidden layers of meaning, to cull from them a story that can orient the mind in the future ... to break the chain of narrative continuity, to shatter chronology as the natural structre of narrative, to stress fragmentariness, historical dead ends, failures, and ruptures" (87, 88). Rather than conservative, totalitarianism according to Arendt seeks to erase all accounts of the past except one and hence in contradistinction, rich traditions have resources to stave off totalitarianism to the extent that they cultivate mulit-layered histories. See Hannah Arendt, *The Origins of Totalitarianism* (New York: Harcourt Brace Jovanovich, 1979).

pitched a tent and lived among us (John 1:14); here innovations follow course in continuity with that which came before; here the new self-shows as honor of the old. The *genuinely* new holds together. Describing how Newsong has held together continuity and innovation, past and future, Pastor Dave Gibbons writes:

> *We're different but not entirely new. Our prayer is that we always show a deference and humility to the previous generations. To be "new" is not the goal but to be Christ-like and adaptive to the Spirit's movements within the myriads of subcultures in a given context. We're firm believers in the movements of embrace as espoused by theologian Miroslav Volf. This embrace is even of our past.*[7]

By tending a common history, and the God common to that history, do Christians come to find that they are gathered around one body as one body. Without that shared history, these other communities cannot help but appear as competitors within the cultural logic of capitalism. Gathered around the one body made available not through competition but offered as gift, the basic economies of these previously rival communities are transformed into a mutual sharing; through this sharing, the respective Christian communities each face different challenges but share a common inheritance through which to negotiate both these challenges and one another at the intersections of these challenges.

The sacramental shape of Christian existence between baptism and the Lord's Supper introduces and instantiates into the world a politics called church by which Asians and Asian Americans, Asian Americans and all Race Americans, and generations across generations share a common life within God's infinite generosity and eternal accommodation. Since God is eternal, there is space within God's life for all these. As the Lutheran theologian Robert Jenson says, "God can,

---

[7] Pastor Dave elaborates on Newsong's on-going relationship with its predecessor Asian immigrant churches: "We from the beginning got the blessing from about 10 of the top Korean first generation pastors both in Seoul and the USA to demonstrate our honoring of the past and respect of traditions/cultures: Dr. David Sang Bok Kim (Hallelujah church), pastor Hah (Onnuri) and Rev. Won Sang Lee (KCPC). We intentionally sought their blessing. We didn't want to be seen as reactionaries but building upon our previous generations. Hence, to this day we still have connections with several key Korean churches in Seoul and locally. In fact, I'm still considered a missionary from Onnuri Church (Seoul) to America. They still send me checks! In fact, I speak at Korean conferences (in Seoul and locally at Sarang here in Anaheim) to affirm our connection." Personal correspondence, October 15, 2009 (Quoted with permission). As I noted in the first lecture, I am uncertain what such a blessing would look like considering the interlacing complexities of Southern California's ethnic ecclesial life. Still, Pastor Dave and Ken Fong of Evergreen certainly demonstrate the integrity necessary for these complexities, even if such integrity cannot preclude the real losses that ensue.

if he chooses, accommodate other persons in his life without distorting that life. God, to state it as boldly as possible, is roomy ... "[8] The divine economy called God's roomy-ness is both metaphysical and pragmatic, speaking on ontological and practical registers. All the nations, *including* all the nations of America, share in the cosmic transformation of God's salvation and in the immanent material performances of that salvation. This means this common sharing is no flaccid multiculturalism, which cordons in zoo-like conditions difference for the sake of difference.[9] Rather, this common sharing is a genuine sharing, a true commonweal.[10] The baptized are initiated into the same body to be the same body; they drink the same blood from the same cup.

Hence Emmanuel Katongole, our Ugandan priest who didn't know he was black until he came to America, describes worship as "wild space" that cannot, with its mutually inhering bodies, but seem unhygienic according to Western standards of sterile individualism.[11] Sharing God's body renders us, as God's body, the visible image of God in the world while simultaneously making visible our particularities that reflect God's created *donum Dei* of difference (God's gift of difference); the one body of Christ makes visible this one body in all its parts. There is no body without its parts. Unlike what has become the case in market economies, these body parts do not compete with one another but are each the conditions of the others' health and wholeness. Hence Asian immigrant Christians and Asian American Christians, Asian Americans Christians and their Christian racial others, theology and the church are *each* parts of one *body*. As Paul quips, feet and hands and ears and eyes are not at cross-purposes with one another: "You are the body *and* individually members of it," Paul writes (1 Cor. 12). We are each Christian and individually Christians. We are each Christian and individually theologians or pastors, Mexican American or Asian immigrant, parents and children. As Father Katongole intones, "If we can begin to see each

---

8 Robert Jenson, *Systematic Theology Volume 1: The Triune God* (Oxford, UK: Oxford University Press, 1997) 236; *Systematic Theology Volume 2: The Works of God* (Oxford, UK: Oxford University Press, 2001), 34.

9 For my critique of multiculturalism, see Jonathan Tran, "The Limits of Franz Boas' Multiculturalism: An Augustinian Critique," *Polygraph 19: An International Journal of Culture and Politics* (No. 19/20, 2008), 55-77.

10 Augustine of Hippo, *The City of God against the Pagans*, ed. R. W. Dyson (Cambridge: Cambridge University Press, 2002), 99, 147-48, 640.

11 Emmanuel Katongole, "Greeting: Beyond Racial Reconciliation," in *The Blackwell Companion to Christian Ethics*, eds. Stanley Hauerwas and Samuel Wells, 68-81 (Oxford: Blackwell Publishing, 2004), 74. For an extended account of the gathering powers of Eucharist, see William Cavanaugh's magnificent *Torture and Eucharist: Theology, Politics and the Body of Christ* (Oxford: Blackwell Publishers, 1998).

other not as strangers in competition for limited resources, but as gifts of a gracious God, then we will already have discovered ourselves within a new imagination, on the road to a new and revolutionary future, which worship both signals and embodies" (81). In other words, holding it all together is, for Christians, worship.

AT THE BORDERLANDS OF ASIAN AMERICA

In preparation for these lectures, I sent a good friend a draft in order to get some feedback. Roger grew up in a first generation Chinese church, left for some time and later returned to another Chinese church with a budding English ministry. As well, he is a veteran team leader of a para-church ministry that serves Asian Americans, and while the ministry is ethnic specific, it prides itself on being open to anyone; in other words, even though his ministry is ethnic-specific, he does not consider it over against. In response to my first lecture, Roger wrote,

> I have to say that as an Asian American attending an Asian church with a struggling young adult group, I felt like I was on the defensive for most of the first lecture. You say strong things, and I know you mean to (and often they are quite good points), but at times I felt like your criticisms were harsh and unfair ... The whole time I read this lecture, I wondered, "Where do you see yourself in this discussion?"

I imagine these words reflect the feelings many Asian Americans might have upon hearing yesterday's lecture. It is not my intention to put people on the defensive, though it is also not my intention to make concessions to avoid that. I have often wondered why it was that Dr. Hertig and the leadership of this symposium invited me of all people to be the keynote speaker for this conference. If I had to guess, it might be my forthrightness and willingness to say things in a way that is forthrightly *un*-Asian American. In other words, given all the work they were putting into getting everyone together, I'm certain they wanted someone interesting and they must have known that as a student of Stanley Hauerwas, I would rather be interesting than right, better to be wrong than boring. So it was for your entertainment that they brought me, and I hope I have at least been entertaining, if not always, or even often, right. But I suspect that there is a deeper reason they brought me here to be with you. I suspect that they see in me Asian American Christianity. Not in the sense that I represent its bright future, for certainly people like Roger do that a whole lot better, but that I represent Asian American Christianity with all of its wrought contradictions, mourning and tragedy, all of its attempts to hold together its over against, leaving behind, and separation from. I imagine they invited me to be the speaker for this historic moment for Asian American Christianity because I embody (however unflatteringly) its story.

I live at the borderlands. (I mean this more than in the sense that I live in central Texas, which from the perspective of you provincial Southern Californians probably seems like the borderland between madness and civilization, between good and evil.) I live where Asian Americans live, at the borderlands, between belonging and not belonging, between home and exile, between Asia and America. I, like many of you, became a Christian in a first generation Asian church. I like many of you no longer attend that church. For nine years, I was involved with InterVarsity Christian Fellowship, four of those years as a student leader, five on staff. Over those years, I saw the fellowship, and hence its character, become increasingly Asian American as the second and third generation showed up on campus and claimed their birthright. Like many of you, I fell in love with Asian America, largely because I identified with it, understood its passions, struggles, questions and desires as my own. In Asian America I found a home. If I had stayed in California, I have little doubt that I would have made my home there, taking up residence in a second and third Asian American church and taking in all that is Asian America in Southern California.

But for many reasons, my wife, Carrie, and I left, and found ourselves of all places in North Carolina where there are less Asians than squirrels. I was among three Asian Americans in three years of seminary. I remember how thrilled I was whenever I passed one of these other Asian folks in the halls, so happy to see someone who looked like me. It didn't matter that I didn't know their names; I felt immediately at home with them. Transient my whole life, I did in North Carolina and later in central Texas what I've always done, make do, hold it together. We made friends with mostly non-Asians, foraged for good Asian food, attended white and black churches, and wondered constantly where and what home was. As an Asian intellectual, I never struggled with what Cornel West describes as the black intellectual's dilemma;[12] never worried to what extent my scholarship either appropriately *addressed* or sufficiently *transcended* my ethnicity as an

---

12 Cornel West, *Keeping Faith: Philosophy and Race in America* (London: Routledge, 1993), 67-88.

Asian American Christian academic, for I worried neither about "my career" nor about my Asian American identity regarding my career. As the last thing Dr. Hauerwas told me before I left grad school, "Jonathan, never be afraid to be yourself." And I knew without doubt, my *self* is Asian American Christian. Though I am one of two minorities in an overwhelmingly white male department, I have never hesitated to remind my colleagues, lest they forget, that I am not white and I have fought hard for the cause of diversity on the faculty. Once, I began the first day of a new class with the assurance to my students, "Don't worry, I speak English." I could tell by the amount of laughter, they had wondered whether I could speak English.

As confidently as I have tried to position myself in my largely white world, I have often felt great loneliness, longing for a place called home. In a very white part of the country, in a very white job where I read white theologians and teach white students while surrounded by white colleagues, often times living in intentional Christian communities with white people, and playing basketball with white guys, attending a white church in what often feels like a white religion, I have sometimes asked myself, "Am I turning white?' I hope not. I hope that I am turning these white places yellow. But unmistakably there is a longing for something that is not over against, something that is not a leaving behind, something that is not separated from what feels like a big part of who I am. In my world, I imagine everyone else feels more at home than I do.[13] I assume that everyone

---

13 For example, as I was completing final revisions for these lectures, I felt compelled to submit the following editorial to Baylor's student newspaper:

> I'm assuming that the Lariat staff vets potential advertisements for messages that would be offensive to the Baylor community or detrimental to Baylor's Christian mission. In other words, it would not knowingly post an ad that, for example, makes racially belittling jokes or openly promotes racism. Either the staff allowed one to slip by, or (more frighteningly) simply does not consider Asians and Asian Americans on this campus worthy of such protections, since the Lariat posted an ad on Thursday, October 29 that was offensive, belittling, and probably stupid: "Stream kung-fu movies from the park, while ditching your Asian Studies class," read the Clear mobile internet advertisement. I've never taken an Asian Studies course though I'm willing to bet the great diversity of Asian cultures cannot be boiled down to watching Jackie Chan clips or Bruce Lee movies. While a novice in Asian Studies, I do teach Christian Ethics here at Baylor and have often applauded the way the Lariat takes seriously its role in shaping Christian minds and bodies for the betterment of the church and the church's place in the world. This ad undercuts those noble purposes. Posting this ad is similar to posting an ad that states, "Gangsta Rap = African American culture" as if the richness of all that is African American culture and history could be reduced to a few asinine media perceptions. Asians and Asian Americans already have to deal with the tired "Asian = Martial Arts" stereotype and the racist slurs that come with it; this ad does not help their cause. Now I realize that Asians and Asian Americans do not warrant political and ethical considerations in this country, but perhaps we as a Christian university might do better, not least because Asians and Asian Americans make up a good percentage of the diverse student body Baylor's always bragging about. I don't expect Clear to do any better, but

else doesn't feel a stranger in a strange land as do Carrie and I, and as I sense my children increasingly will. Is what I long for to be surrounded by Asian Americans the way I am surrounded by white folks?

In some ways, for sure. In the same ways that many of our very good friends are Asian Americans from other parts of the country, we long to live in those parts of the U.S. In the same way that we used to be affirmed and encouraged in Asian churches and esteemed as Asian leaders and mentors, we long for a place where we don't have to prove ourselves given white people's low expectations of Asian American Christians. To the extent that in Waco people believe Asian equals Chinese, I would love to live in places like Southern California where there is not only a diversity of ethnicities, but as importantly, a diversity of ways of being Asian American. And certainly to the extent that I think some of the most interesting and amazing things happening in American Christianity are happening in churches like Newsong and Evergreen, I would love to be a part of those church communities.[14] And yes in the ways in which according to Texans, good Asian food is constituted by a buffet and cellophane wrapped almond cookies, I would love to live near a Sam Woo.

These are longings and fears and hurts that you as an Asian American can only know if you've lived in a place like Waco. These are the longings nurtured by a childhood lived outside the ambit of Asian community, of a biting loneliness of growing up without Asian friends, with the deep scars of racism, an adolescence that was saved from itself only when at age 16 I first stepped into the world-affirming world of the Chinese Baptist Church of Orange County and discovered Asian America and Christianity in the same moment.

And so those who wonder where I see myself given the critiques I freely level against Asian American Christianity should have no doubt, I am Asian American through and through and understand as well as any in this room what it means to stand betwixt and between Asia and America.[15] And I celebrate through and

---

I do expect the Lariat to do much better.

14 I would be remiss if I didn't mention that 90 miles from Waco, in Austin, TX no less, Pastor Gideon Tsang has developed one of the most unique young Asian American churches in the nation. See www.voxveniae.com. Gideon, like many of our young Asian American pastors, possesses an impressive array of skills and passions. For a time, alongside pastoring Vox Veniae, he took over preaching duties at Waco's University Baptist Church when his good friend Pastor Kyle Lake passed away unexpectedly. UBC is internationally renown for featuring the Dave Crowder Band, which demonstrates the range of Gideon's gifts and appeal.

15 I borrow this phrase from Peter C. Phan, "Betwixt and Between: Doing Theology with Memory and Imagination" in *Journey at the Margin: Toward Autobiographical Theology in American-Asian Perspective*, eds. Peter C. Phan and Jung Young Lee, 113-133 (Collegeville: The Liturgical Press, 1999). Also see the splendid collection of essays, *Realizing the America of Our Hearts:*

through being Asian American and will fiercely defend its goodness and integrity as if defending my very identity. My critique is but a vigorous defense of what I consider the extraordinary gift of Asian American Christianity, and, to quote Amy Tan, "it may look worthless, but it comes from afar, and carries with it all my good intentions."[16] I, like many of you in this room, am Asian American Christianity. We are its desires, its hopes and frustrations, its paradoxes and failures, its exodus and its homecoming. God created us Asian American just as God made us Christian. Our Christianity reminds us of the goodness of being Asian American, and being Asian American reminds us what it means to be Christian, to be between homes, to be strangers in strange lands, betwixt and between, holding it together, pilgrims on the way somewhere.

IMMIGRATION AS PILGRIMAGE

As I was saying yesterday, Asian Americans have been quick, too quick, to relinquish their identity with Asian immigrants. Yesterday I talked about the consequences that had for our relationships with our Asian immigrant forebears, regarding the racial modes of violence we enact against Asians and sometimes even against our own bodies. This violence is part of becoming American, since becoming American has come to mean passing into whiteness by shedding certain things. I also said this was framed by a second bind, that while we so desperately want to be American, America will not allow it, seeing us as outsiders. Asian Americans enact the violence necessary to be American, but are considered forever foreigners within America.[17] In this way, the Asian American is neither Asian nor American. She sits at the borderland between, forever leaving Asia and forever arriving in America, not allowed home in either place. This is the state of pilgrimage.

As lamentable as this position may be, I believe it has the potential to be the future of Christianity in America. The betwixt and between status of Asian Americans — that they have both left homes and yet are still not at home, that they hold simultaneously two identities at once, that their allegiances are constantly contested, that they are seen by the world, as Michelle Kwan was seen by that

---

Theological Voices of Asian Americans, eds. Fumitaka Matsuoka and Eleazar S. Fernandez (New York: Chalice, 2003).

16 Amy Tan, *The Joy Luck Club* (New York: Ivy Books, 1995), 3-4.

17 Mia Tuan, *Forever Foreigners or Honorary Whites: The Asian Ethnic Experience Today* (New Brunswick: Rutgers University Press, 1998).

reputable newspaper, as consummate outsiders — is finally a very good thing. It has the potential to be the future because this betwixt and between status is itself *the* status of Christianity in America. The Asian American church has the very real ability to remind Christianity it is not at home in America. Rather like Asian immigrants, Christians come from another place and are on their way to another place. Though they live here, this is not their home. They are on their way, pilgrims as it were according to Augustine. We are temporary here, and hence, rather than building homes in America, we like Jesus and Paul after him pitch tents in this place, becoming tent makers in a land through which we are only passing.[18] To be sure, the pilgrim status of the church does not exempt it from political engagement, social concern, and relational commitment, but it does mean that what the church works toward is not directed by the idioms determined by the temporal order but instead an eschatological hope in and patience of the world. Against the now tired charges of sectarianism, pilgrimage maximally affirms the material goodness of the earthly city (in all of its political, social and relational specificity) by calling it to its eternal consummation.

What a thing it would be if upon identifying yourself as American, someone asked you, "But where are you really from" because the goodness of your life seemed so foreign. Christians in America, like Asian Americans in America, are not home, having left, having immigrated, having been exiled. Like the African American church before it, the Asian American church can challenge the vast cultural accommodation that has become American Christianity. The African American church knows America is not its home, since black people have too often become the "wretched of the earth" (to use Franz Fanon's phrase[19]) as they are reminded on a daily basis in racist America. And so the African American church has been the on-going proclamation to African Americans that they are not granted full citizenship in America because they are citizens of another country. According to African American folklore, as portrayed beautifully in Toni Morrison's *Song of Solomon*, at the worst moments of slavery, the African would sprout wings taken away during the middle passage and fly home.[20] Folktales

---

18 For an account of Christian existence as pilgrimage, see Gerald W. Schlabach, "Deuteronomic or Constantinian: What Is the Most Basic Problem for Christian Social Ethics?," *The Wisdom of the Cross: Essays in Honor of John Howard Yoder*, ed. Chris K. Huebner, Harry J. Huebner, Mark Thiessen Nation Stanley Hauerwas (Grand Rapids, MI: Eerdmans, 1999), 449-471.

19 Franz Fanon, *The Wretched of the Earth* (New York: Grove, 2005).

20 Toni Morrison, *Song of Solomon* (New York: Vintage, 2004). Also see Sandra Adell's essay "Modernism in the Afro-American Studies Classroom" in *Approaches to Teaching the Novels of Toni Morrison*, eds. Nellie Y. McKay and Kathryn Earle, 63-72 (The Modern Language Association of

like this became the living subtext of their stories in the new world.

At its worst, Asian American Christianity sets itself over against, leaves behind, and separates from as part of an idolatrous attempt to establish a home in America. Tired of longing, fearful of not belonging, humiliated and exiled, they give up the pilgrimage of faithfulness for an acclimation to comfort. They of course are not alone in this; it is America's great pathos to conflate Christianity with security and as Americans, we Asian American Christians are not immune to this. Instead of honoring and protecting the great gift of our wanderings, rather than cherish, celebrate, and even evangelize our exodus, we have set ourselves up in barricaded homes in the manicured suburbs of America's great loneliness. In this we have become white, for the over against, the leaving behind, and the separation from is what you do as you pass into whiteness.

It need not be this way. But in order for it not to be this way, we will have to learn to embrace, not relinquish, our status as outsiders. We Christians will be forever foreigners until we come to that place where "God will be the end of our desires. He will be seen without end, loved without stint, praised without weariness..." to quote *City of God*.[21] Until then, Asian American Christians have the ability to remind the church in America that pilgrimage while difficult can also be life giving. What makes Asian American Christians aliens is not their racial identity finally but their faith, and their racial identity has the ability to inform that faith, to situate it betwixt and between. The Asian American lack of belonging can become an index for *Christian* lack of belonging.

Here we might begin to see anew the struggles of the first generation church and find in their difficulties a paragon of the Christian life. Here we might take our cues not from the ones that leave, but the ones that stay and fight the good fight until it is finished. Here we begin to lean into the courage of the mutual indwelling, the holding it together, of Asian and Asian American Christian community life. We will have to learn from all those brave souls holding it together. They are over exhausted and under resourced. They rarely make headlines, except as empty churches in the great wake of the Silent Exodus. Their churches are often called "old-school" and "out-dated," even "dying." They feel caught between obeisance to one generation and the squeaky-wheel needs of the next. They are

---

America: 1997); and Virginia Hamilton, *The People Could Fly: American Black Folktales* (New York: Knopf, 1985), 171.

21 Augustine, *City of God*, 1179.

regularly punished for their faithfulness, silenced because of their vision.

I think here of all those ever-shrinking youth groups and their tireless leaders. I think of their on going struggles to create innovative ministries all the while the first-generation Korean pastor can't figure out why the *Jdsn* doesn't show up to 6:00 AM morning prayer every day. Balancing the lives of their youth between overbearing parents and an imperializing MTV culture, they hold it together if holding it together means the lengths of their efforts. I think of Campus Crusade students who return from schools like Stanford or Harvard, who, by the creativity of their vision, see in their old-school, out-dated, dying churches fertile soil for new things. Bless their hearts, though they have the gifts to lead anywhere, they lead here. They see huge increases every year, as people learn to rethink the workplace or be more accountable with their money. True, few new people ever join these small communities and their numbers remain meager, but then again, who cares when you're seeing *this* kind of growth? And of course I think of the English pastor, having given everything for a congregation that grows smaller by the week. He realizes that with his entangled commitments to the Vietnamese-speaking congregation he cannot compete with the mega-church down the street. He's okay with that since he knows faithfulness to the gospel is enough to worry about for one day. And so he and all these brave souls go on, holding together what others consider not worth holding together. Here the goods of faithfulness are their own good, reminding us of the end toward which our pilgrimage is directed. Quoting Augustine's *City of God* again: "Here we shall rest and see, see and love, love and praise. Behold what will be, in the end to which there shall be no end!"[22]

CLAIMING THEOLOGY AS BIRTHRIGHT

In Genesis 27, Jacob steals the blessing Isaac intends for Esau. Unlike God's blessings, Isaac's blessings are finite; there is but the one birthright, which Jacob decides to take for himself under the guile of a rather hairy disguise. I think this strange story rings true to the tradition of theology within Christianity. What is different is that the tradition of theology, as it passes through the historical church, is God's gift through the Spirit as the mediator of the revealed word of God. In this way, like the Spirit, it is not finite, and it's issuance, God's giving of blessings, denotes a plenitude that cannot be exhausted and hence needs not be fought over; in other words, God's blessing is not scarce and so no competi-

---

[22] Ibid., 1182.

tion need ensue around it. Rather than fought over, theology as a blessing is something that must be passed on and claimed. This passing on and claiming requires both forebears gracious enough to bequeath and recipients grateful enough to inherit. Without this dual activity, blessings go nowhere. In the Esau and Jacob story around Isaac's blessing, clearly something goes wrong in the passing on/receiving and grace/gratitude process.

Something, as well, has gone wrong in the passing on of theology within the contemporary American church such that the suspicions that surround academic theology mirror the suspicions and subterfuge of Jacob and Esau around Isaac's blessing. The church postures itself in a highly defensive relationship to theology, feeling the need to guard its doors against the haters and heterodox, seeing theology as fundamentally undermining the very real, very important practical needs of day to day church life. The Christian academy in turn looks askance on the church, with a tendency to discount those real, important, and practical concerns. Much of the conflict centers around the very right concerns of orthodoxy, regarding reading and living around the scriptures faithfully. The church believes it is already doing this such that theology feels like redundant interference. As well, the academy believes orthodoxy is its sole concern and so positions itself superior to the church. Much of this I believe has to do with a gross failure on the part of many theologians in understanding that they work in service to the church. Any theology that does not serve the church in its important, real, and practical concerns is simply not theology.

Despite the many failings of contemporary Christian theology, there is still much that is rich and right about it; there is much about contemporary theology that does indeed see itself as serving the church. Indeed, a quick review of the guild's top journals (*Modern Theology*, *Pro Ecclesia*, *New Blackfriars*, the *Journal of the Society of Christian Ethics*, etc.) and many of the top publishers of academic theology (Eerdmans, Cascade, Blackwell, SCM, Brazos, IVP, etc.) shows the Christian academy going to great pains to produce scholarship for the church. Unfortunately not all of it escapes the black hole of the incomprehensible or boring, but the effort is there. And *then* there is much that is very comprehensible and very interesting, written for church congregants invested in the important, real, and practical theological concerns of the church, since on their best behavior, theologians are nothing other than church congregants invested in the important, real, and practical concerns of the church.

Theology is a birthright the Asian American church must claim. I believe academic theology has the potential, over the next few years, to be the single greatest help to the Asian American church in its mission. The whole enterprise of getting right our speech about God as a form of worship called theology is the inheritance of the Asian American church, which stands within, not outside of, this long line and must receive this tradition and see itself as a critical part of its conversation. If not, it will forfeit a blessing that God makes abundantly available to the church universal. The best theology is doxology, worship of God and hence internal to the best practices of the Christian church. And it has to be this language, the language of doxological worship in its specifications as biblical studies, church history, theology and ethics that must be the language of the Asian American church. This does not mean that this language is the only discourse the church participates in; it is not theological discourse over against business discourse but rather theological discourse as the interpreter of secular discourse, theological language as a middle language between church and world.

Theology is not the exclusive province of white Christianity. No doubt some very important theology developed within the context of white European Christianity, but theology is not white. Theology is not white because God is not white and theology is about God. Nor were our greatest theologians white, and here I mean Justin Martyr and the Cappadocians including Macrina and Maximus the Confessor, Catherine of Sienna and St. Thomas Aquinas, Teresa of Avilla, Luther and Calvin and the like. In the same way that these brothers and sisters sit squarely within the tradition of theology, so do Asian Americans. When we do theology we Asian Americans sit at the table with Maximus and Teresa and Luther; we like they are honored guests as we feast together on scripture as revelation of the Triune God.

The tradition of theology is our tradition. We like Esau and Jacob should seek this blessing as if our whole life depends on it, something worth wrestling over; it is God's good gift of God's Spirit in time. Theological language, the church's wonderfully fascinating history, the tools of biblical exegesis, all this should be part of our common language. As we Asian Americans become less ethnically Chinese or Vietnamese, and as we leave Tagalong and Korean behind, we just might find a common language in the language of theology. Better yet to loosen theology from the dominance of white Christianity by learning to read theology in the native languages of Tagalong or Korean, allowing it, as all good theology should, to be restated and reworked within the local languages to which it, as servant, must answer.[23] How wonderful it would be if our congregants were equally familiar with the Christological debates of the fourth and fifth century as they are with recent health care debates, as adept with the biblical languages as they are with Spanish and Vietnamese, because as we all know, the Christological debates and the health care debates and the languages of Greek, Spanish, and Vietnamese are all about God. How wonderful if our high school students were as adept in pneumatology as they are in biology. Asian Americans consistently prove themselves as top students in the social sciences, the humanities, and yes, of course the sciences, math, and all those classes that make up the golden path to medical school. Why not theology? English is a foreign language for Asians; theology need not be. Our excellence and competency in theology ought to reflect theology as our inheritance, as we participate as invited guests to this great banquet.[24] As Pastor Kevin Doi says, "It feels good just to be included and heard because we have been neglected and ignored until now. I think that it is important that we embrace our identities as Asian Americans and also engage with the larger culture. To do so, we need to have a voice from our context." One of my friends, Ken, who is a youth pastor here in Southern California, has his middle and high school kids learning theology from day one, has them thinking through doctrine, asks them to invest as arduously in divinity as they already do in AP Calculus and SAT preparation. He takes them seriously by taking seriously that their minds were made for the theological task of loving God.

It strikes me that the Asian American church in Southern California and Fuller Theological Seminary today meet at a critical juncture, "directed toward a future goodness that transcends the current ability to understand what it is," to quote Lear again. The question seems to be whether Fuller can speak the language of theology appropriate to the context of the Asian American church and whether the Asian American church will be able to attend its ears sufficiently to hear. "The future goodness" of the Asian American church's faithfulness "transcends" their individual abilities, but together, Fuller and these churches give each other their best shot.

---

23 Consider political theorist Sheldon S. Wolin's conception of tending in *The Presence of the Past: Essays on the State and the Constitution* (Baltimore: The Johns Hopkins Press, 1989), 90-91.

24 For a survey of recent Asian American theology, see Jonathan Y. Tan, *Introducing Asian American Theologies* (New York: Orbis, 2008) and my review in *Religious Studies Review* (Vol. 25, No.1, March 2009), 46-47.

Until this happens at places like Fuller or Trinity or Gordon Conwell, seminary professors will go on doing what they have always done: see white people when they see Asian Americans, and they will continue to teach Asian Americans as if their uniquely created identities and contexts do not matter, and then they will always see Asian Americans and Asian American churches as just lesser versions of white Christianity. If this continues to happen, and if we Asian Americans keep getting trained like white Christians and white ministers, then our ministries will always be merely lesser, ripped-off copies of white Christianity. This will not only be a curse to us, but a curse to white Christianity, which needs its non-white brothers and sisters to intervene on its hegemony; just as the worst thing we can do is to allow Asian American Christianity to wallow in the supremacy of white Christianity, so the worst thing we can do is leave white Christians to wallow in the supremacy of white Christianity. As soon as Asian Christianity steps up and claims it birthright, the sooner theology in this country will begin to move away from its white center. White Christianity and white theology will be made yellow, and its mythic purity and its political capital will give way to humble service in the church. In this way is Asian American Christianity the future, because, like it's black and Latino sisters and brothers, it has the potential to drastically change the landscape of contemporary Christian theology.

YELLOW CHRISTIANITY

Let me conclude these lectures with some remarks on color. The ascension of the Asian American church and the development of its distinct voice and vision can be thought of as a declension of white Christianity, just as the color yellow might be considered a substrate of the color white — less pure, a lesser primary; *yellow* can look like a dirty white. In this way, Asian American Christianity has resembled a second-order white Christianity. And in many ways Asian American Christianity has been a yellowish adaptation of white Christianity, taking its cues from white churches and denominations, looking to white preachers, evangelists, and missionaries for its theological voice, tuning into white worship, turning to white biblical commentators and following in the footsteps of white ministry leaders. None of this is bad, for we share the one body of Christ. But this *becomes* bad when that body gets construed as white, which it often has for Asian American Christianity. Asian American Christians in this way are different than their African American sisters and brothers. African American Christianity historically developed on its own terms, since European missionaries did not designate

Africa a place worthy of evangelization, choosing instead to enslave Africans. Nor did the African American church in America receive the resources of white Christianity, because white churches were historically unwilling to share the blessings of Christianity with their enslaved or segregated fellow Christians. In this way, black Christianity largely developed on its own, developing its own theology, its own worship and preaching styles, its own visions of God and leadership, so on and so forth.[25] Black Christianity is no lesser version of white Christianity. It is as authentically Christian as white Christianity; no more contextualized, no less syncretistic. In this way, it is both a challenge and a gift to white Christianity.

I believe Asian American Christianity can so be a gift to its other Christian brothers and sisters. I see Asian American Christianity not as a lesser version of Christianity but just plain ol' Christianity. It is one version of Christianity among others. As such, it has the remarkable ability to deeply influence. Specifically in relation to white Christianity, Asian American Christianity has the potential not of being a tainted shade of white Christianity, but indeed of making white Christianity something else entirely. Asian American Christianity can make white Christianity yellow. The ascension of Asian American Christianity, like the development of the black church before and the Latino church alongside, can upset the logic of white purity, infusing into the whiteness of American Christianity hues and flavors and textures that will leave American Christianity a truer reflection of America, and a truer reflection of Christianity. This yellowing effect will transform Christianity because it will allow the church to more fully enter into the fullness of God's gathered body, which is not yellow or white or black, but indeed yellow *and* white *and* black, holding together that which only God's church can hold together.[26]

---

[25] Winthrop D. Jordan, *The White Man's Burden: Historical Origins of Racism in the United States* (Oxford: Oxford University Press, 1974), 11. According to Jordan, evangelizing the Africans would first require seeing them as worthy of salvation, a notion Europeans could ill afford if they were to enslave them. Also see Albert J. Raboteau, *Canaan Land: A Religious History of African Americans* (Oxford: Oxford University Press, 2001).

[26] I am indebted to the following people for reviewing and commenting upon drafts of these lectures: Young Lee Hertig, Jonathan Wu, Roger Lam, Carrie Tran, Michael Tai, Lindsay Cleveland, Jerry Park, Maria Cheung, and Ken Hsu.

RESPONSE #1

Response to Jonathan Tran

BY **MIYOUNG YOON HAMMER**
FULLER THEOLOGICAL SEMINARY

I would like to thank Dr. Lee Hertig for inviting me to participate on this panel. And to Dr. Tran, thank you for your challenging and necessary words. I found that much of what you said resonated with my own experiences and thoughts. And in many ways I feel that I am more of a case study of what you're talking about than a resident expert in the socio-political-theological ideas that are expressed in your talk.

I would like to begin by briefly sharing about myself as my response to Dr. Tran's lecture can only be understood within the context of who I am as a person. I'm a second generation Korean American woman. I grew up attending a Korean church that was more of my extended family than simply a church family for we had no other family in the United States. The church had an active English ministry program that continues to thrive, Some of the elements of success that Peter Cha (2007) refers to in his chapter, "Constructing new intergenerational ties, cultures, and identities among Korean American Christians" remind me of the church in which I grew up. For example, the social, spiritual, and fiscal ownership that the English ministry (EM) congregants have taken of their church and the mutual respect that is given between the Korean ministry (KM) and EM church leaders have been instrumental in the success of the church overall. Whenever I visit the church, I am impressed to see how well the EM has flourished amidst many seasons of transition.

In my own faith journey, however, I have arrived at a different place from where I began. In the last five years, my husband and I have been part of the Anglican Church. Among other things, we are drawn to the liturgical worship, the sacramental perspective, and the recitation of creeds. And as I honestly reflect upon this journey, it is clear to me that being in the Anglican church has much more to do with my and my husband's conviction to attend a liturgical church than it has to do with not being in an Asian American (AA) church. And while I feel at home at the Korean church in a way that I never feel "at home" in any other church, I have chosen to be where I am based on faith tradition rather than ethnic cultural tradition.

Response #1: Response to Jonathan Tran

The little that I've shared about myself directly relates to the two themes that emerged for me in Dr. Tran's talk. In the section titled *"An Over Against"*, Dr. Tran states:

> "This over against will leave us each thinking that we are now left to fend for ourselves, that we are not part of something bigger, which in consequence only inflates our sense of our own bigness in our own individual big heads. We don't seek to learn and partner with others because we keep forgetting there are others. We don't commingle with others because we have learned to understand our identity not as a mutual gathering but an over against."

Here, I understood Dr. Tran to be talking about AA churches in the context of a society that segregates rather than communes and integrates.

I would like to offer a reframe of this isolated, insular image of the AA church. The perhaps unintended function, but profound benefit, which I believe is an example of God's faithfulness, of the AA Christian church for first generation immigrants is to provide a place of healing and belonging in addition to spiritual nourishment. For example, I have never attended a Korean church that did not serve potluck at the end of every service. During potluck, people are at once physically and emotionally fed and church life comes alive. This church life provides opportunities for congregants to participate in community life in a way that they do not otherwise experience. So many of our immigrant parents gave up their status when they came to America. Physicians became liquor storeowners and those who once wore suits became the ones who dry-cleaned others' suits. It is in the church that members have status as elders and deacons and for many, it is one of the only place where they have a sense of place, dignity, and respect.

The Korean church that I grew up in was more than a place of worship for my family. Beyond being a spiritual home, it was our extended family and a place of belonging amidst the psychological homelessness that plagued my immigrant parents as well as many of their peers. It was one of the only places in our family life where there was a profound sense of solidarity and connection that in many ways provided healing for the feelings of displacement and loneliness that was so common for immigrants like my parents. I'm reminded of the phrase, *la cultu-*

ra cura: the curing culture. This refers to more than healing rituals and traditions that are embedded in one's culture. More importantly, in my mind, it refers to the healing and curing that comes from simply being among your own and having a sense of belonging and connection in your own culture. This is not to imply that church merely functions as a social club or community center. At the center of it all, the Gospel and all the ministries of the church should, of course, flow from the central truth of the Gospel.

This reframe, if you will, is important to keep in mind if we want to talk about a way to preserve AA churches in a meaningful way. We need to acknowledge and understand the multiple values within the AA church, namely: the value of intergenerational reconciliation and healing, the value of spiritual nurturance, the value of preserving and passing down traditions, and the value of providing cultural solidarity. Here, we can honor both the value of the AA church as cultural safe haven of the first generation congregants while exploring ways to make the church meaningful and positive for subsequent generations as well.

Now I would like to move onto the second issue which, for me, relates directly to my own faith journey. A significant issue that Dr. Tran touches upon, that I believe deserves further exploration, is the extent to which the phenomena that Dr. Tran observes in the AA church parallel current trends in the broader evangelical church. As a marriage and family therapist, I am trained to think contextually and to conceptualize issues in systemic terms. Thus, examining different systems and understanding how they, perhaps, operate in parallel process helps me make sense of the complex dynamics while providing information about how to work with and within those systems.

In the section titled, *A Separation From*, Dr. Tran talks about the business model of the emerging AA church and the ways in which "AA Christianity mimics White Christianity." Dr. Tran discusses ways that AA Christianity is in lockstep with the broader evangelical church by, to put it simply, tending to favor innovation over tradition when it comes to modes of worship and ways of doing ministry. The cultural critic and commentator, Ken Meyers, host of the audio journal Mars Hill Audio, has a lot to say about the issue of tradition and history in the church. From the 76th volume released in 2005, he references a number of scholars on this very topic. From the late Collin Gunten, he quotes,

> ... *tradition involves a personal relatedness to others in both past and future time. To deny the salutary character of tradition is to say that we*

can only be ourselves by freeing ourselves from others by suppressing the other rather than being set free by them.

Further, he references theologian Steven R. Holmes,

> *Because of the doctrine of creation, historical locatedness is something good. The tradition we inherit is part of our location in history and so in doing theology it is necessary to relate to the tradition.*

And finally, D.H. Williams,

> *The growing indifference of the free church and especially non-denominational congregations to the founding period of the church's understanding of orthodox belief threatened to result in growing subjectivism in theology. Bereft of historical points of reference of accommodating the church to a pseudo-Christian culture such that the uniqueness of the Christian identity is quietly and unintentionally traded away in the name of effective ministry.*

Here, these scholars were not and are not necessarily talking about the AA church and yet their words and their meanings resonate with Dr. Tran's critique. First and foremost, it is imperative that we understand the AA church as being located within a larger system that is in parallel process. Perhaps recognizing this parallel is one way to make the AA church relevant to the Christian academy who, according to Dr. Tran, considers the AA church to be irrelevant. It is important to examine the parallels between AA churches and the broader evangelical church in America. We must understand that the AA church is not isolated but rather is connected to the larger evangelical church that is dealing with some of the same challenges of stepping away from its history in an effort to make church relevant to the current generation. In family systems terms, when one part of a system is affected, all other parts are affected, much like a mobile. Thus, we cannot afford to understand our situation and seek out a solution without recognizing the role the AA church plays in the larger evangelical community and vice versa.

In closing, reading through Dr. Tran's talk and preparing my response conjured up more questions than answers. In what ways are other non-AA churches grappling with these same issues? Is there a way to be unified as one body in our efforts without losing our unique identities? Is there such a thing as AA Christianity apart from White European Christianity? If so, what does that look like? I would take it a step further and ask, is there such a thing as Asian Christianity apart from White European Christianity? How does a community of believers retain their cultural identity through traditions, values, and practices while holding firmly to the traditions, values, and practices of the Christian faith? How do we approach this as both/and as opposed to either/or without distilling either part?

RESPONSE #2
Response to Jonathan Tran

BY **CHARLENE JIN LEE**
SAN FRANCISCO THEOLOGICAL SEMINARY

I wish to respond to this morning's lecture by offering limited explorations on two concerns: the first one, Dr. Tran's concern about a lack of a generative Asian American theology; a second concern that I see as missing but needful in this discussion, a gender analysis of an emerging Asian American theology.

Dr. Tran posits that the future of Asian American Christianity rests on the Asian American church's readiness to claim her theological agency. The church's readiness to articulate her particular understanding of God revealed in the record of Scripture, to describe her experience of God dwelling among the often schizophrenic self- and political- identities — floating somewhere between belonging and exclusion; readiness to illumine a prophetic imagination of God whose vastness sustains humility in all theological articulations. Claiming this theological agency as a church connected to a complicated slice of the human community we've named Asian American, means to take a seat at the table of theological discourse and to announce a theology.

It has been long recognized — at least I hope I am right about this assessment — that it is presumptuous to speak of Theology (with a capital "T"), as if there were only one, as if there were a canon of orthodoxy that prescribed how human persons are to know God.[1] It has almost become cliché to talk about the relationship between one's *locus theologicus* and one's beliefs about God; to talk about how the place from which we read the world affects how we read the Word. Yet, I am suspicious that in some ways these ideas of the multi-sitedness of theology have been nothing more than an exercise in cordial welcome of diversity. Christian theological discourse at large has and has had at its center a canon of theory, described by western — namely European, namely White,

---

1   My *Mujerista* sisters are to receive credit for teaching me the heuristic frame I apply in the paper for naming the discourse between Theology/orthodoxy and the struggle for legitimizing theologies. For amplification, see particularly, Ada Maria Isasi-Diaz, "A Platform of Original Voices," in Leon Howell and Vivian Lindermayer, eds., *Ethics in the present Tense: Readings from Christianity to Crisis* (New York, NY: Friendship, 1991); "*Mujerista* Narratives: Creating a New Heaven and a New Earth," in Margaret Farley and Serena Jones, eds., Liberating Eschatology: Essays in Honor of Letty M. Russell (Louisville, KY: Westminster John Knox, 1999); *En La Lucha* Continues (Maryknoll, NY: Orbis, 2004).

Response #2: Response to Jonathan Tran

namely male — voices. Theolog*ies* emerging from different places, described by different voices are assigned to peripheral positions.

Imagine with me the seating assignment, or arrangement, around the table of theological discourse. The table is fairly large, I would say. Many of the seats have been taken up and warmed for a long time — for centuries, in fact — by the same people. And we study them; in our courses we assign textbooks and ask you to write papers that seek to understand their conversations. You and I might find an open seat at this table, and we may be hesitant to speak. For it may take some time to figure out what they are talking about — for they, those guys who've been warming up those seats, have established a lingo, a way of thinking, a way of being that is unfamiliar to us. We sit quietly saying to ourselves, "Wow, we have so much to learn about theology." Allow me to remind you here that "they" are not owners of theology. Theology does not belong to one language (one way of speaking) nor to one set of categories. We have mistakenly assumed the center as if it were the original point of view. Paul exhorts: Don't be so proud. Don't be so proud to think that you are entitled to a seat at the table. "The original branches were broken off, and you, a wild olive shoot, were grafted in their place to share the rich root of the olive tree" (Rom 11:17). Those at the center of the theological discourse, to whom we assign the dominant position, are a wild olive shoot. So are we who feel like we're the newly arrived foreigners trying to fit in and nervously formulating something worthwhile to say. All of us around the table are unintended guests, equally not belonging, but by grace invited. It can only be with gratitude and humility that any one of us engages in theological inquiry. It can only be that we look to one another for mutual dialogue and not by the hierarchical categories assigned by the sociopolitical histories that have shaped a lopsided power dynamic.

Dr. Tran's call for a generative Asian American theology has indeed been met by theologians invested in carving out a space for a seat at the table. Most of this space, however, has been taken up by a descriptive theology. Describing our non-prominent position, the marginal position in light of the center position filled by — as Dr. Tran names it — White Christianity. Google marginal, margin, marginalization and Asian American Theology/Christianity, and you will find plenty to read and to learn. Dr. Tran, in his lecture, describes the invisibility of Asian American Christianity and asks for mainstream Christianity and its organizations, like the North American evangelical seminaries, to pay some attention to our presence and to our voice. I think we have named and described our marginality for a long time. I am anxious to see us move from a descriptive theology to a constructive theology that debunks the mistaken assumptions about the seating assignments and invites others to a kind of theologizing that is marked by a posture of humility and gratitude. Precisely the kind of theologizing that does not rely on an over and against paradigm.

Perhaps, what we need is a theological Copernican revolution: to realize that we do not exist as an accessory orbiting around this Theology (with a capital "T), but that all theologies (born out of the stories of all people spoken in language that seems "non- theological") and all people are actually orbiting as the miniscule planets around the true center: God. And perhaps, this more accurate rearrangement of the theological landscape is the constructive hope we can offer to those at the center and to those struggling at the margins in the present paradigm.

Indeed, if we truly embraced the "roomy-ness" of God, we can be generous with one another, and we can take the risk of maintaining each of our assertions as provisional to the extent that someone else, theologizing from a different place may offer an insightful understanding of God's vastness that we could never know or imagine from where we are.

I wish to respond now with my preliminary reading of this lecture, as a North American woman of Korean heritage.

Dr. Tran, I, too know a little bit about living in the borderlands. Like those whom you praise for returning to their roots, to the ethnic church of their parents, I have stuck it out in the first generation immigrant church. When I first entered ministry, I was determined to learn the story of my cultural faith heritage. I served on a staff of 30 pastors, of whom only 3 were women. Yes, I had to wake up while it was still dark and cold to make it to early morning services, and yes, I had to sit in very long staff meetings where the senior pastor spoke most of its duration. However, I gained from there the color of my spirituality and learned the faith language of Christ's body converged with the Korean culture. Yet, there were parameters set for the shape of my ministry. I could not envision fully becoming and growing within the confines of an overtly genderized church culture. At staff gatherings, my seat was assigned with the pastors' wives and with the other three female pastors. You will be proud that I stayed, that I have served in variations of these arrangements in other first generation and second generation congregations in the different regions of the United States that my

Response #2: Response to Jonathan Tran

life and learning pursuits had taken me. I was always only a partial version of me in these churches. But I was there. Your call for me to faithfully return, to reattach is overbearing.

The church that is most home to me today is not the Korean church, not the Asian church, it is not the Asian American church. It is the church where I am asked to preach — no, not only to the children or to the youth — to the whole church, where I am invited to teach at men's weekly meetings, where I am asked to pray with the sick, and where I help to serve communion. There are no more good Korean meals to look forward to after service, and I coerce my husband to drive out to LA for some spicy *soon doo boo* on Sunday evenings, after a long day, a long week, of being with my White sisters and brothers. But, I am more fully me in such a church; I am more fully becoming a faithful one called to serve the church. Then, there comes the Sunday, when after speaking in the morning worship, a cousin of a congregation member visiting from

Texas rushes over to shake my hand, and with her bright and hard fuschia acrylic nails digging into my small hands, says: "Why, I think it is just wonderful that you've learned to speak English without an accent!" Like so many of you, I live in the borderlands.

Yearning to find stable place, to be understood, to belong, yet always knowing that I will never quite belong fully. Yet, I choose not to defer to a center that seeks to assign me my place, but to constructively be me — growing in and out of my awkwardness and gaining strength to my voice. Realizing that, while I don't know how to hold it together, I am being held together.

I offer a tiny glimpse into my personal narrative to ask all of you, now charged with the responsibility to claim your theological agency as the Asian American church, and to ask our speaker to consider who is at your table? The table where this contextual, constructive, beautiful Asian American theology will emerge and flourish? If it is to be contextual, constructive, and beautiful, it must take the risk of inviting threatening bodies who will slow down the process by asking new questions, uncomfortable questions, and problematize whatever picture you had of an emerging Asian American theology. Are you willing to see and to loosen the rigid structures of your Theology that inform the polity and ethos of your churches? Are you willing to image God and to speak and teach of God as beyond male? And to image the ministry of God and theological agency entrusted to all made in God's image? Are you prepared to critically examine the malebodiedness of your pastoral staff, of your sessions, your elders, your leaders? Are you prepared to widen the circle of your Theology and open the invisible gates in your churches to invite unintended, complex voices that might disturb and make messy whatever neat categories you've knowingly or unknowingly established? I hope to hear a resounding "yes!" someday; I will joyfully return to take my seat at the table beside you, sharing your humility and gratitude, and together stand in awe at the roomy-ness of Grace.

RESPONSE #3

Response to Miyoung Yoon Hammer and Charlene Jin Lee

BY **JONATHAN TRAN**
BAYLOR UNIVERSITY

First, many thanks to the panel for what I thought were incisive and beautiful responses and corrections to my lectures. For Professor Yoon Hammer and the first panel, I have no response, for to argue with their comments would be to suggest that somehow they were not absolutely right; as well, to respond at this point would be to suggest that this is about who's right and who's wrong instead of engendering a certain kind of conversation. So I am grateful for the care of the panel's important arguments, especially the way Professor Yoon Hammer attends to the critical modes of healing made possible by Asian and Asian American churches. Just as Rev. Dr. Michael Lee rightly pointed to a lacuna within my lectures, so she filled out that glaring void by describing the crucial role social gatherings play in the life of immigrant and minority Americans. As well, I am grateful for the narrative she offers of her own faith life and the ways it highlights the vitality of traditional liturgies for the formation of theological character and imagination.

I *would* like to respond to Professor Jin Lee's comments as they raise issues that my lectures inadequately addressed and hence show an important failing on my part. We are indebted to Professor Jin Lee for reminding us of the central place gender must take if these conversations are to go forward in a productive, and as she says constructive, manner. As I said last night, the Holy Spirit is God's imagination poured out on the earth (following John Milbank), and it is by God's Spirit that the future is made available by the Spirit's aeration of time, by opening fissures in our closures, fragments in our totalities, a way forward amidst our various disjunctions. I believe that for the Asian American church the question of difference opens at the site of gender identity, equity, and formation. I think God is very interested in how the Asian American church will respond to these questions.

Professor Jin Lee duly states that my words become "overbearing" to the extent that my admonitions that Asian American churches retain fidelity to the first generation does not pay heed to the plight of Asian American women in these churches. As she relates her own pilgrimage she describes how her attempt to hold together generations resulted in first generation Korean Christians assigning her to child care and spousal support, this despite her academic and ministerial training, and I would argue, clear brilliance as minister, teacher and theologian.

Here, I should take a moment to clarify a point my lectures failed to make explicit, a point that many of the panelists picked up on. I am not saying that it is unfaithful for Asian American Christians to leave first generation immigrant Asian churches in order to start second and third generation Asian American churches like Newsong or Evergreen. I am not saying it is wrong to leave. I am not saying that faithfulness demands one stick it out no matter the circumstances. I need to be clear here because, as many of you who have suffered this can attest, these questions are not simply academic. Hence, I am not suggesting leaving is unfaithful. I am suggesting that leaving may be unfaithful. I am not suggesting that one must stay. I am suggesting that one can stay. For me the problem is not leaving, but rather the suggestion that leaving is our only option. Rather than sacrificing ourselves on the horns of staying or leaving, I want to resist choosing between those two as if we have no other choices. If we parse the issue as if leaving means innovation and staying means faithfulness, we ignore the ways staying may indeed be incredibly innovative and leaving mightily faithful. Even though, as I state in the lectures, leaving often means relinquishing the sources of moral deliberation, that does not mean that staying necessarily honors the past, for as many of us know, there are many who stay who in no way honor the past. Likewise, there are ways of leaving that do honor the past and do so in unexpected and innovative ways that speak to, again invoking Lear, "a future goodness that transcends our current ability to understand."

By asserting that leaving may be unfaithful, and by showing *how* that might be the case, I am trying to interject an intervention, a stopgap if you will, in a powerful trajectory that asserts leaving as the only option we have. What I am beseeching is that we take time to consider all the options God, as the Lord of history, has made presently available to us. As I said in beginning these lectures, we need to step into the impulse to dream amidst the crushing homogenization the world of totalitarianism forces upon us. In order to do so, we need to inhabit God's temporal roominess and consider our options, of which "staying" or "leaving" are only two among many others.

The problem here is the same ethical limitations of any account of "Christian realism" that forgets the Chalcedonian affirmation of Christ's full, and real, humanity and divinity. Ignoring the reality of Christ's humanity, war becomes necessary because we have no other options, a mode of thinking that is a complete failure of theological imagination. For me, the thinking "We're being threatened so we must go to war" is the same Christologically impoverished thinking as "We're being oppressed by the first generation congregation and so must leave this church." Surely God in Christ makes possible more options, and if God doesn't then we are surely doomed. In the same way that war has become the de facto response to threats to America, so leaving has become the de facto response to generational issues in the Asian church. Yet war and leaving are both unimaginably destructive, and most immediately destructive of theological imagination because it refuses to take the time God gives the Church to imagine a different world.

Imagine if the resources poured into developing intercontinental stealth bombers and more efficient automatic weapons were invested in considering options other than war. Imagine if following 9/11 America responded to the murderous acts of a few heretical Muslims by bombing Afghan Muslims (who already think the West is hell-bent on destruction) with bread rather than bombs. Now imagine if we took all the creative energies that nourished the development of churches like Newsong and tried to imagine creative ways to get along with first generation congregations. I realize that these options can't but seem unrealistic and even irresponsible but what bothers me is that we rarely consider them because of the mad dash desperation that has rendered them, without thought, unrealistic and irresponsible. God gives us more time and imagination than that. God demands more time and imagination than that.

So I am not saying leaving Asian churches is unfaithful; I am saying it may be unfaithful; I am saying we can stay. Amidst the great torrential rush to get out and start new churches that always suspiciously look like Newsong or Evergreen, I am trying to turn our attention to other options that have been rendered invisible by the mad dash of the Silent Exodus. Some of these other-ed options include staying and trying to imagine ways of holding together. Here I take Rev. Dr. Michael Lee's Young Nak as instructive of just such a possibility. Young Nak's success needs to be broadcast and celebrated with the same exuberant hopefulness as are other successes, some of which do include leaving; doing so will enrich our imagination and expand our choices beyond the horns of a self-imposed Scylla and Charybdis. And if we need to leave, we had better as well pay attention to the consequences and mourn the absence of reconciliation that often inhabits and encourages leaving. Even if we cannot achieve reconciliation, we need to display the appropriate contrition, and to be sure, contrition doesn't mean pointing fingers.

I think my restatement only further emphasizes the import of Dr. Jin Lee's comments. I will confess that as she offered her de/constructive appraisal, I kept thinking to myself, "Gee, I wish I had said it so well." In her critical comments, Professor Jin Lee states that my lectures would have her return to the oppressive environment that would crush the many gifts she and many other Asian American women embody and offer. Yet as I have just tried to clarify, I am not trying to castigate her to the silence such churches often impose. I am asking all of us to imagine the relationship between first generation Asian immigrant churches and Asian American Christians — a relationship played out at critical junctures like gender — beyond the narrow axis of leaving or staying. If we remain beholden to these bewitching linguistic habits, we will continue to, as Wittgenstein notes, bang our heads against the fly bottle.

Professor Jin Lee perspicaciously and powerfully relates how leaving the first generation Korean church freed her to faithfully live into her calling as minister and professor. Another way of underscoring that is to remind ourselves that if she did not leave, we may not have her tremendous and tremendously efficacious presence before us today. Yet, how do we pay witness to the goodness of that departure without disparaging the goodness of the many women who stay? How do we describe honestly the injustice of the church's gendered presumptions about spousal support and childcare without belittling the great and powerful vocations of spousal support and childcare? In order to do these well, we will need to move beyond the paradigm that suggest leaving is our only option. If we do not, we will not be able to avoid portraying those women who stay as somehow second-class women, a portrayal I believe, and I imagine Dr. Jin Lee believes, not only dishonors many of our mothers, wives, sisters, and daughters, but as well dishonors Christ whose sacrificial death reveals the servant nature of God, rendering spousal support and childcare the upshot of Christian discipleship and hence the vocations of all Christians.[1]

---

[1] See Amy Laura Hall's "Naming the Risen Lord: Embodied Discipleship and Masculinity" in *The Blackwell Companion to Christian Ethics*, eds. Stanley Hauerwas and Samuel Wells, 68-81 (Oxford: Blackwell Publishing, 2004), 82-49 and Sarah Coakley, *Powers and Submissions: Spirituality,*

Professor Jin Lee is absolutely right that my lectures inappropriately articulated these kinds of realities and hence became oppressive and overbearing. For that I apologize.[2] It is inexcusable omission, for which I feel (the right kind of) shame. Thank you for naming my blindness; I consider your insight and admonition a great gift, as I am profoundly susceptible to the very closures I am trying to describe. I mourn the reality that many churches and Christians, including many in this room, cannot honor your ministry and your many gifts, and I apologize for the ways my lectures have deepened that dishonor.

I do believe that the oppression of women in the first generation Asian church is cause for leaving. Unfortunately, I don't imagine that is often named as a reason for leaving by those who leave, who tend to repeat these dishonors in innovative new ways. But I also do not think that such oppression means we must leave, and if we do leave, in leaving we need to take stock of what we are leaving and grieve those losses, which would include damning those first generation congregations to their patriarchy. It is true that in staying, it is highly unlikely first generation churches will witness and cultivate the broad array of gifts women bring to the table; yet it is equally true that in leaving, in taking those gifts out of the sightlines of those churches, it is equally unlikely they will ever see them. I believe that honoring the past that makes our lives possible, and the past that makes the future possible, requires we attend to these kinds of realities and expand the range of options God makes infinitely available to us.[3]

Philosophy, and Gender (Oxford: Blackwell, 2002), 3-39. See also Coakley's "Does Kenosis Rest on a Mistake? Three Kentoic Models in Patristic Exegesis" in *Exploring Kenotic Christology: The Self-Giving of God* ed. C. Stephen Evans, 246-264 (Oxford: Oxford University Press, 2006), her "The Woman at the Altar: Cosmological Disturbances or Gender Submission?" in *Anglican Theological Review* (Vol. 86, No. 1), 75-93, and Hall's *Conceiving Parenthood: American Protestantism and the Spirit of Reproduction* (Grand Rapids: Eerdmans, 2008). For my considerations on parenthood, see Jonathan Tran, "The Otherness of Children as a Hint of an Outside: Michel Foucault, Richard Yates, and Karl Barth on Suburban Life," *Theology & Sexuality* (Vol. 15, No. 2, 2009), 191-211.

2 Once again, the thought of Hannah Arendt proves instructive. For Arendt, the plurality of action requires the covenantal rudiments of promise and forgiveness. Seyla Benhabib's reading here is especially apropos: "The interminable and inexhaustibly intricate horizon of human affairs yields certain consequences: first, in acting there is always a necessary disjunction between intention and consequence. Not only are our actions always open to the reading and misreading of others, but also 'because of this already existing web of human relationships, with its innumerable, conflicting wills and intentions … action almost never achieves its purpose' (HC, p. 184). Second, action is immersed in this medium of stories it 'produces,' 'as naturally as fabrication produces tangible things' (HC, p. 184). Actions are indentified by their doers as well as by the spectators and those who suffer their consequences through various narrative tellings, and in this way they become part of the 'web' of human affairs. 'I thought I was being generous,' I say, 'whereas you thought I was being overbearing and protective' … Such is the web of narratives within which human affairs unfold." Seyla Benhabib, *The Reluctant Modernism of Hannah Arendt* (Oxford: Rowman & Littlefield, 2003), 113.

3 Many thanks to both Professors Yoon Hammer and Jin Lee for permission to include their remarks here and for continuing conversations.

RESPONSE #4
Response to Jonathan Tran

BY **KEN FONG**
EVERGREEN BAPTIST CHURCH, LOS ANGELES

Let me begin by saying how humbling it was to learn that my work at the Evergreen Baptist Church of LA (Rosemead, CA) since 1978 was included in Dr. Tran's important presentation on the future of the Asian American Church. Of the panel of five respondents, I was the only one whose ministry was subjected to the keen and critical eye of Baylor's Tran. So my response to his first lecture will focus on the section in which he critiques EBCLA.

In his second section "A Leaving Behind," Tran revisits Helen Lee's article in *Christianity Today* (August 1996), which chronicled the ongoing mass departures of more assimilated and acculturated Asian American youth and young adults from immigrant Christian churches. Tran brings the saga up to date, expanding on the reasons for this 'Silent Exodus.' Motivated primarily by growing desires to find or found churches that more closely matched their emerging Americanized sensibilities and preferences, large numbers of disaffected Asian and Asian American Christian youth and young adults have been leaving the first generation language churches. Tran then describes pan-Asian American churches like Dave Gibbons' Newsong (Irvine, CA) and EBCLA as being both catalytic agents and clear beneficiaries of this sociological trend. While he clearly admires the pioneering work of these trendsetting churches, Tran is gravely concerned that taking what appears to be the path of least resistance is causing generations of Asian American pastors and Christians to leave behind critical pieces of their heritage and culture, including the priceless stories of the faithfulness of their pioneering predecessors and their trustworthy God.

Twenty-plus years ago, I fully admit that this would be both a fair description of the mindset of the leaders of EBCLA. During the birth and rapid popularity of the Church Growth Movement throughout the decade of the Eighties, we were convinced that we could strategically position ourselves to be beneficiaries of an anticipated new homogenous unit: Americanized Asian Americans. Making this the focus of my Fuller dissertation, I took note of clear demographic trends amongst the prevalent Asian groups on the West Coast. The Japanese American community, due in large part to their unique and painful position in American

Response #4: Response to Jonathan Tran

history, was in what I called the "vanguard position" among all Asian groups in America in regard to assimilating and acculturating to the dominant American culture.[1] American Born Chinese (ABCs) were already dating and marrying Japanese American friends with increasing regularity and much of EBCLA's numerical 'growth' during that decade was at the expense of established Chinese-language churches. We didn't see this trend ever reversing. Instead, we saw the formation of an honest-to-goodness Asian American people group, a fusion of Americanized Japanese- and Chinese-Americans. It didn't take a genius to predict that in the foreseeable future, Americanized Korean-Americans and eventually other Americanized API-Americans would one day join the Silent Exodus, too. We were determined to create the kind of church that would be a better fit for them, even if it meant leaving behind most of everyone's past in the relentless quest for a new future.

A funny thing happened on the way to that future. I joined the board of InterVarsity Christian Fellowship USA and went to my very first Urbana Student Missions Conference in December 1990. I was confronted with a holy God who called us all to be uncomfortable for the sake of overlooked and the forgotten. And I was confronted with a gospel that wasn't about capitalizing on sociological trends but about becoming a corporate, concrete witness to the gospel's unmatched power to reconcile disparate and desperate people.

As I began to dive deeper into the uncharted waters of this much more uncomfortable but much more redemptive future, I became increasingly convicted that EBCLA's future must include first generation Asian bilingual immigrants as well as non-Asian Americans. It must include not just the educated and the very educated but the less educated as well. It must include the up-and-comers as well as the down-and-outers. It was no longer going to be about what is most convenient, efficient, expedient or even comfortable. It was going to be about becoming a living laboratory of the power of the One who has destroyed every wall that divides to create, in and through himself, one new humanity (Eph. 2).

As the mid-nineties approached, that compelling vision began to dominate my vision for our ministry. But at least two-thirds of our church was perfectly fine with the original homogenous vision that I had cast. They couldn't openly refute it without sounding like a bunch of self-centered Christians. However, when the

---

1 For more on this and how my outlook on the future of Asian American churches later evolved to include multi-ethnicity, see my Pursuing the Pearl (Valley Forge, PA: Judson Press, 1999).

senior pastor announced that God's Spirit had revealed to him that it was time to make two churches out of us, that two-thirds went with him. Those who remained behind with me were either gung ho about this more redemptive future or just too attached to the current church campus.

That was 1997. We have seen many people come and go since then, but the bulk of the church today appears more on board than ever before. Like Newsong (Irvine) we are a unique buffet of at least a dozen different API groups, plus just about everybody else, e.g., White, Black, Mexican, Native American, multi-ethnic. However, we have a much wider age-spread, ranging from infants to nonagenarians. We are a church that was planted in 1925 to reach Japanese-speaking immigrants in East Los Angeles; Newsong was planted a little more than a decade ago as a pan-Asian American, multiethnic new church. They host thousands of people each Sunday using the latest and greatest high-tech methods of communication and presentation; we host less than 700 weekly, using fairly basic methods and tools that enable us to connect people better to God's presence and God's gospel. I have no idea how many first generation Asians attend Newsong, but at EBCLA, roughly 15% of us are Asian immigrants. However, what's unusual is that the first generation folks are typically young adults or younger, and the leaders are, in the main, either second or third generation people. So as we learn to embrace these 1Gen folks, we are also learning to embrace and incorporate their native cultures and sensibilities.

In sort of an odd, upside down way, we are trying to live out the very "stay home" dynamic that he asserts is critical to the Asian American Church having a substantial future. Lately, we've gone out of our way to honor the oldest members of EBCLA by having them share their wrenching stories of deep faith in Christ amidst untold hardships and injustices. This past spring, I conceived and directed a unique conversation among three generations of EBCLA leaders. Calling upon the now-88-year-old Japanese American former pastor of this church and a young thirty-something Caucasian church deacon, we engaged in a spirited cross-generational conversation about the past, present, and future of EBCLA. While the four cameras recorded this historic conversation,[2] I coaxed the retired pastor not only to share about the really tough decisions the leaders faced in the 1950s but also his opinion of what's going on now and where it appears God is taking us. We both thanked him and his generation's leaders for

---

2 Entitled "The Heroes' Journey," this 3-part DVD is available for purchase. Send a request and a check (payable to EBCLA) for $10 to: Evergreen Baptist Church of LA, 1255 San Gabriel Blvd, Rosemead, CA 91770.

Response #4: Response to Jonathan Tran

making some really tough decisions, some of which we're still benefiting from today![3] Then the retired pastor and I turned to the young deacon and asked her what her generation needs us to do or decide today to lay the groundwork for what God's Spirit has formed in their hearts, things that we older leaders may not see now or be able to imagine.

I don't believe it's possible to send most Asian American Christians back to first generation churches. But I am convinced that it's possible to move forward together toward the future that God has prepared for us, being deliberate to show that we're all standing on the broad shoulders of our faith-progenitors and -pioneers. While I don't believe it's possible to build a solid future by returning to our roots, I do believe that we can build a sustainable and sound future if we strengthen our roots to our pasts.

When asked to describe how this works at EBCLA, I like to use the metaphor of a restaurant that has evolved along with its customers. Evergreen LA started out as a little Japanese restaurant in East LA. Its menus were all in Japanese, the owners and the cook were from Japan and they only served simple but authentic Japanese food. Understandably, the only ones who frequented it in those early years were Japanese-speaking immigrants. As time went on, the proprietors and the regulars got married and started families. Their children loved going to Café Evergreen. They could sort of read the menus but they certainly loved the Japanese food. As the range of their preferred foods kept pace with their own acculturation, they occasionally wished that the restaurant would diversify its menu a bit. They were delighted one day to find some new additions like pork fried rice, egg foo young, and steamed pork hash with salted fish. By the 1970s, many of the second generation folks had become young adults and they began to bring a smattering of their Chinese American friends and dates to Café Evergreen. As more Americanized Chinese started coming, the Japanese-American owners and cooks began adding more and more Chinese dishes to their once Japanese-only menu. Today, in keeping pace with its ever-diversifying clientele, Café E has broadened its menu to include fried chicken, tamales, pho, chicken adobo, and durian-laced jello. Ownership and the cooks have kept diversifying along with

---

3   Just a few years removed from the injustices and hardships of the concentration camps during World War II, the Japanese American leaders of EBCLA chose to change the name from "Nisei Baptist" to "Evergreen Baptist" to appeal to future generations of Japanese Americans. They also voted to separate from the Japanese-speaking members, helping them move across the street to be a new, language-based church.

the menu, too. The head chef today is a third generation Chinese American married to a third generation Japanese American. Restaurant critics today are raving about the unique fusion of ingredients, tastes, and textures that have become the unique offering of this now-eighty-four-year-old eatery that relocated to Rosemead in 1985. But if you look carefully inside your taco or your roast beef sandwich, you'll likely find a bit of tofu.

RESPONSE #5

Response to Jonathan Tran:
Theological Imagining with Asian American Churches

BY **RICHARD MOUW**
FULLER THEOLOGICAL SEMINARY

It's been a great day for us. We're so delighted and honored that this kind of conversation is happening, and that it's happening here at Fuller Seminary. We have a lot to learn, and that learning process was greatly advanced today, I assure you of that.

I was glad to be asked to talk only very briefly this evening about how we might work together in imagining the future contribution of Asian American churches to the role of theological education here in North America.

That idea of imagination is a very important one for us to reflect upon. Several months ago my good friend Craig Dykstra of the Lilly Endowment wrote a wonderful essay for *The Christian Century* in which he talked about the importance of theological imagination.[1] He began by saying that in his work with lawyers he has come to see that "they have been formed — by their legal education and even more by their years of professional work in the law — in a particular way of seeing and thinking that is distinctive to that profession." He observed that they have developed a "legal imagination." And a legal imagination consists of "a penetrating way of knowing that enables really good lawyers to notice things, understand things, and do things that others of us simply cannot see or do."

That idea, that an imagination of a certain sort helps us to see certain things, to understand certain things that may not be available to other people, is very important in the context of our discussion here today. The Christian church in North America needs an Asian American theological imagination. And you are the experts in this area.

I say that remembering a time that at an alumni gathering we were addressed by an African American graduate of Fuller who had gone on to have a very distinguished academic career in a very short period of time. He had become very successful in the secular academy. And he told us this:

---

1   Craig Dykstra, "Imagination and the Pastoral Life," *The Christian Century*, March 8, 2008, pp. 26-31.

Response #5: Response to Jonathan Tran: Theological Imagining ...

When I was at Fuller, I was always the black guy up in the back part of the class who never said anything. I never felt like I had a voice at Fuller Seminary except on one occasion. It was an occasion in which we were being taught about urban theology and the professor asked each of us to prepare a brief report in which we reflected theologically on the neighborhoods in which we were raised. For the only time at Fuller Seminary I was the theological expert in that class, and I had a theological voice.

This is an important kind of theological reflection, and it requires the kind of theological imagination that can only be grounded in the experience of knowing who you are and where you have been. This kind of theological reflection depends on knowing what has formed you and shaped you, and pursuing those reflections for the sake of the whole church of Jesus Christ.

One of the books that's been most influential in my own theological thinking is by the Japanese American theologian Kosuke Koyama, *Water Buffalo Theology*.[2] Koyama had been raised in Japan, he did his undergraduate work in Japan, came to the United States for graduate work, went back to Tokyo, and then was sent by his church to be a missionary to Northern Thailand. He said, as someone who has spent his life thus far in urban Tokyo and in New York City suddenly to find myself in the rural regions of Northern Thailand was a bracing and shocking experience. He told of being a missionary that was supposed to bring the gospel to the rural residents of Northern Thailand, most of them Buddhists. He asked the Lord, "How in the world am I going to preach the gospel to these people?" He remembers driving around the countryside on his motor scooter and seeing people standing up to their hips in rice patties alongside of water buffalo. He prayed further to God, "How do I bring good news to people who spend part of the year up to their hips in rice patties alongside of water buffalo and the rest of the year hiding from the monsoon rains?"

He decided to read the Bible imagining himself standing alongside of the water buffalo in a rice patty. With that imaginative posture and location, he found things in the Bible that he had never noticed before — for example, that there's a lot of stuff about water in the Bible, and God's relationship to water. God is the Lord of the rains, that He is the Sovereign One who sends the rains in accor-

---

2 Kosuke Koyama, *Water Buffalo Theology* (London: SCM Press, 1974; revised edition: Maryknoll, NY: Orbis Books, 1999).

dance with His own sovereign purposes. The Lord our God is above the floods, He's above the rains, He's above the rice patties. And one piece of good news, he said, is that there's somebody in the universe who's dry! But he developed a very rich understanding of what it meant to bring the Gospel to the residents of Northern Thailand with a profound sense of imagination. This only came from actually standing in the rice patties and reflecting theologically on the message of the Scriptures as it is addressed to that cultural context.

At the end of the book he describes his methodology thusly: As a missionary, he was sandwiched between two realities and engaging in a two-directional exegesis. He was exegeting the culture of the rice patty — the questions and answers that emerged out of standing alongside of water buffalo and rice patties. But he was also exegeting the Scriptures in the light of the questions and answers that emerged out of the rice patty. That's not just a missionary thing. That's true for all of us, whatever our area of ministry, and it's certainly an important part of equipping men and women for ministry in an institution of theological education like this. We need constantly to be engaging in that two-directional exegesis that includes exegeting culture.

There is a challenge for Fuller Theological Seminary as it thinks about what it means to equip women and men for ministries, specifically in the Asian American context — and I heard all of the nuances today about using that kind of terminology, but I also heard that it was okay to use it. As Fuller attempts to equip women and men for ministry in the Asian American context, it's so important that we get a lot of help in exegeting the culture, and the cultural experiences, and also in reading the Word in the light of the experiences of first and second and third and fourth generation Asian Americans. You here specifically have the gift of being sandwiched between the migration experience, the experience of cultural dislocation, cultural relocation, the experience of understanding the realities confronted by different generations who have been impacted by the migration experience. You are in a place to exegete the questions and answers that we must bring to the Word of God and to other theological traditions in order to effectively minister in the cause of the Gospel.

Yesterday I spoke at the ordination of one of our Chinese — actually mainland Chinese — students who had graduated from Fuller and was ordained yesterday in a local Lutheran congregation. And at dinner we were talking and I said, "What are you learning in ministry about the unique challenges of the Chinese American community?" He said, "I'm learning that in ministry in the Chinese

Response #5: Response to Jonathan Tran: Theological Imagining ...

American community there are two things we have to address: the one is materialism, and the second is fragmentation." By "fragmentation" he meant an afflicted sense of consciousness that comes from being thrust into many different, conflicting roles and demands.

This is also true for those of us in the various Caucasian communities — Scotch-Irish, and Dutch Americans like myself. And the ways in which those challenges and those difficulties emerge in different cultural contexts will differ from situation to situation. We need a lot of help in thinking about what it means to minister to people who stand up to their hips in the culture of the North American marketplace, North American political life, North American family life, and many other areas of life. We need you to teach us about who you are, and also teach us about who we are.

In our own continuing attempts to think theologically about these matters I've been much helped in recent years by the discovery of a very intriguing document from the early church titled *The Epistle to Diagnetes*. The scholars don't know exactly when this lengthy letter was written or who wrote it, but we do know that it was composed not long after the apostolic period. It was written by a Christian who wanted to explain to a non-Christian, probably an important official in the Roman empire, the beliefs and practices of this emerging new religion that claims to follow Jesus Christ.

There's one passage in that letter that I especially like. The writer is explaining to this Roman official how Christians understand their roles as citizens of the societies in which they live. He offers this profound comment, "For Christians, every foreign country is our homeland, and every homeland is a foreign country." That's a profound statement about identity. Those of us who have been raised in the religion of Americanism very much need to be reminded who we are and to be taught who we are, what our true identity is. And who can best remind and teach us but those very people who have experienced some degree of alienation from the very culture that many of us have been conditioned to take for granted. We need to be told over and over again that every foreign country is our homeland, and every homeland is for us a foreign country.

I want to conclude with a very strong emphasis on the fact that our true identity is not the identity dictated by our nation of origin, or by our gender, or ethnicity, or by our participation in a certain class of society. Our true identity is that we belong to Jesus Christ. Right now my favorite TV program is *Flash Forward*.

And I like that image, on *Flash Forward* they sit around — some of you know the story — they've all gotten this very brief glimpse of something that's going to happen in the future. And they sit around debating whether it's really going to happen or not.

But you know that in the Scriptures we get a flash forward that really is going to happen. That flash forward is this: that someday we will gather before the throne of God, as a people from every tribe and tongue and nation of the earth, and we'll sing that great hymn of Revelation 5 where, having found the Lamb who is able to open the scroll and to break its seals, the courts of heaven break out into this hymn:

> *Worthy art thou, O Lord, to take the scroll and to open its seals, for You were slain. By Your blood You ransomed men and women for God from every tribe and tongue and people and nation and You have made us a kingdom and priests unto our God.*

We couldn't do it on our own. God in Jesus Christ through the blood of Calvary has done something to us and for us that we could never do for ourselves, not only having saved us individually from our sins but incorporating us into a global community drawn from every tribe and tongue and people and nation of the earth. That's our true identity. So whatever your Asian origin, or whatever you're non-Asian origin this evening, we're kinfolk, we're brothers and sisters in Christ.

That same book of Revelation tells us that at the very end people will march into the holy city from every tribe and tongue and nation and will bring with them the honor and the glory of the nations. So important for us to remember who we are. As Jonathan Tran put it so well today, when you give up the generation that produced you, you have also given up the grounds by which you are able to see well, to morally understand what is happening, and to pay heed to the realities around you.

We need together to engage in a theological imagination that instructs each of us, not only about our cultural context, and not only forms in us a community of memory so that we remember where we have come from, and where the Lord has brought us, from and to, but also who we are as brothers and sisters in Jesus Christ drawn from tribes and tongues and nations of the earth. I hope you "flash forward" and keep that picture in your mind because it's crucial to the kind of theological imagination in which we must all engage.

AFTERWORD
Imagining Asian American Theological Formation and Social Capital

BY **YOUNG LEE HERTIG**
INSTITUTE FOR THE STUDY OF ASIAN AMERICAN CHRISTIANITY (ISAAC)

Gleaning from the Jewish American scholar Hannah Arendt, Jonathan Tran names his fear of triple departures of the Asian American church: "over against" non-Asian American Christians, "leaving behind" its first generation forebears, "separated from" the theological tradition. The way I heard Tran's triple departures was what Werner Erhard names, "completing with the past" regardless of eventually "staying" or "leaving" the immigrant church. I doubt if there is such a thing as "completing" with the past" but it may be possible to identify with the past fully enough that when one departs from it, one cannot avoid "mourning" his or/her departure, as noted by Tran. This mournful departure from the immigrant church is quite different from abandoning the past.

Although it may sound unrealistic, I am nevertheless attracted to the notion of "completing the past" when it comes to the questions of Asian American ministry. I yearn desperately to see new questions raised rather than recycling the same questions for more than three decades. Perhaps, even a semi-closure with the past would suffice by creating a space to mourn our past collectively without juxtaposing "healing" and "belonging" — this is what Yoon Hammer mentions as the "spiritual nourishment" of the Korean American church's potluck after worship.

According to Erhard, when one completes with their past, creating a new future, "not shaped by the past" is possible.[1] Obviously Erhard does not argue that one has to forget their past but rather asserts the importance of not being stuck in the limitations of the past narratives. I resonate with Erhard's naming of "being stuck in the limitations of the past narratives." In this regard, Tran's emphasis on "mourning the loss of the past" is crucial for anyone to move into future possibilities that are *not bounded* by but *resourced* by the past. Tran's reflection on Arendt's point puts is directly:

---

[1] Peter Block quotes Werner Erhard and refers it to "The Erhard Insights: The Power of Language, Context, and Possibility" in his book *Community: The Structure of Belonging*. San Francisco, Berrett-Koehler Publishers, Inc., 2008, P. 16.

> *The past bestows a community the resources to know how to negotiate the unknowable future, to chart a course when the past is always vanishing.*[2]

Tran's fear for the Asian American church has everything to do with the vanishing past. Like the undocumented migrants, Asian American narratives of church history and ministry has not been documented and included in color-blind seminaries' curricula. Perhaps, many Asian Americans remain oblivious to what they are departing from except their own individual experiences of brokenness in the local church. Intellectually undocumented, the future generation will lack resources to negotiate the unknowable future. Transmitting the legacies of the older generation will, indeed, ease identity crisis that the hybrid generations undergo. Definitely, as Tran put it, fighting for theological birthright is much needed.

Likewise, many Asian American women pioneers, feeling parachuted from nowhere to a neverland, find ourselves deprived of such resources to negotiate with life's challenges let alone to be guided to future directions. We also face gendered and racialized resource barriers from both our own ethnic churches and from the mainstream Christian institutions. In preparing for the inaugural AAES from a third space, the barriers I experienced were lack of access to Asian American church pulpits of both the ethnic language speaking congregations and English-speaking congregations. Hence, the reality of tribalized resources hit hard. Alternatively, church women had to organize an alternative space (Mama's Pasadena) to hold a Prayer Banquet and mobilized Asian American community through cooking — Korean BBQ and home-made fusion Kimchi. Where there is rice, AA people gathers and shares our common symbolic identity. Yoon Hammer says,

> *I have never attended a Korean church that did not serve potluck at the end of every service. During potluck, people are at once physically and emotionally fed and church life comes alive."*[3]

---

2 Jonathan Tran's lecture, p. 15

3 Miyoung Yoon Hammer is an assistant Professor at the School of Psychology at Fuller Theological Seminary.

In sharing meals, church becomes a source of "healing" and "belonging" said Yoon Hammer. When leaving the immigrant church, it is the ethnic food and table fellowship that they miss. In case of Evergreen Baptist Church LA, the food evolved along the diversification of Asian Pacific Islanders' constituencies — API fusion buffet with "a bit of tofu" in every menu, says Ken Fong. Also, history is repeating itself with the new immigrants in the midst of 2nd, 3rd, and even 4th generation API members at the Evergreen Baptist Church LA. Obviously people of color connect deeply with table fellowship as Jesus often was going to and from the meals. Undoubtedly food symbolizes rich ethnicities and hence a sense of belonging.

Speaking of table, Professor Charlene Jin Lee offers a fascinating topographic analysis of "seating arrangement or assignment" of theological table. Jin-Lee raises critical questions as to who are at the table and who are not, and how long they have been warming up the seats, and thus who are the "owners of theological table." She calls forth humility and grace in rearranging the seating arrangements at the theological table if we were to construct AA theologies. In departing from the Korean immigrant church, Jin Lee also misses spicy Korean food served in the church. Now that she chose gender equality over ethnicity, she "coerces" her husband to go and grab *soon doo boo* (spicy tofu soup) after serving at a Caucasian congregation.

IMAGINING AN ASIAN AMERICAN THEOLOGICAL CONSTRUCTION

Although "God is roomy," Asian American consciousness has not entered into the theological palace despite Asian Americans being among the largest constituencies that compose all major seminaries' student population and increasing number of faculty. As Jin-Lee offered insightful topographic analysis of the theological table, we were reminded that often, the seating arrangements can be challenging. For such reasons and the fact that we lack a mentor like Mordecai, the scattered and unformed Asian American seminarians have, for too long, lined up like beauty contestants in the theological palace. What would theological formation process look like if we were to have our Mordecais who unlocked Queen Esther's imagination?

Theological formation *of* Asian American churches, *by* Asian American churches, with Asian American churches await to be unleashed. We could curtail perpetual pioneering and thus the silent exodus of our pastoral leaders. And in fact, we will be able to enter into the theological palace not merely as decorative beauty contestants but as theological patriots. As the queen Esther hosted series of banquets, ironically, many panelists at the Asian American Equipping Symposium also used food in describing ethnic churches.

In organizing AA communities as active theological patriots, Peter Block's concepts are helpful: 1) Asian American social capital (assets, resources, and talents); 2) associational life (groups of people voluntarily coming together to do some good); 3) the power of context (past, present and future).

Block asserts that until the group completes its past narratives, their vision for the future is limited. For this reason, Jonathan Tran's excellent articulation of Asian American past and future is significant. Without completing our past narratives, the Asian American Christian community will continue to recycle the same struggles decade after decade. In theological formation process, many seminarians perpetually raise the same old questions from the 1980s, 1990s, and the 21st century. Our Mordecai has been fixated with the culture they left behind in Asia while their offspring assimilate through education in white schools, which leaves them with mere symbolic ethnicities through foods, and implicit emotions rooted in their family upbringing. As long as they are left with the sink or swim approach, with no bridges to the past and the future, the chances of transformation are remote. From hearing at least three-decades old questions and frustrations, the AAES was created to "connect the dots" of the Asian American Christian community's assets, resources, and talents, this in partnership with Fuller Theological Seminary.

Charlene Jin Lee, elaborating on Tran's point that "God is roomy," also articulated the importance of moving from "descriptive theology" to "constructive theology." Her theological topographic analysis of "seating assignments, or arrangement at the table of theological discourse" offered the direction and vision for our 2nd annual Asian American Equipping Symposium. Just as God is roomy, the table is fairly large, says Jin Lee. She describes the history of the table:

> Many of the seats have been taken up and warmed for a long time — for centuries, in fact-by the same people ... We are not owners of theology ... Perhaps what we need is a theological Copernican revolution.

Hence, we have been "floating somewhere between belonging and exclusion," as Jin Lee put it. She offered "constructive hope" that may secure our seats at the table both in theological discourse and gender discourse. Jin Lee decided to forego sitting at the sidelines in Korean ethnic churches and chose a mainstream church space where she is one of the key players at the table, although this meant missing spicy Korean dishes after church. Charlene Jin Lee, like Miyoung Yoon Hammer, chose a gender inclusive mainstream church to express her full voice as a woman. When confronted with the choice between ethnicity and gender inclusion, many minority women understandably tend to choose gender inclusion. For the future of Asian American churches, generational separation and gender exclusion may minimize the experience of the fullness of the body of Christ (1 Corinthians 12).

Another barrier to constructing an Asian American theology includes overcoming our own internalized "isms" that elevate "the owners of theological table" at our own expense. Assured by the vastness of God, we can respect everyone one at the table, not just the "owners of theology." The Israelites had to wander 40 years after exiting from Egyptian rule. Perhaps, we have waited long enough from the sidelines of the table or absence from the table to join the table. When sitting at the table, we will have to reclaim those who pioneered and persevered in making their way through the door from the outside.

Surely, all the Symposium participants appreciated President Richard J. Mouw and his gracious participation in our dialog. The voices of the participants echoed that they all felt included at the table, not overlooked. Have we begun the "yellowing" of Christianity for a truer reflection of America and truer reflection of Christianity toward fullness of God's gathered body as Tran concluded in his lecture? In this fuller body of Christ, I imagine several generations, Asian American women sitting at the table side by side, not at the sidelines. Consequently, I imagine yellowing of Christianity, and Asian American women and younger generations integrating ethnicity and Christianity rather than having to depart from the church-home of nourishing foods to fully exercise their God-given gifts.

According to Robert Putnam's definition[4] of social capital (the cohesion, interdependence, and sense of belonging), Asian Americans possess an extraordinary number of assets, resources, and talents, but they as people are regretfully

---

4   Robert Putnam. *Social Capital and Civic Engagement.* Putnam's analysis on social capital and civic engagement offers much insight to Asian American theological formation in regards to Asian American community's assets, resources, and talents. When AA community's social capital becomes adhesive cohesion, enormous potential for theological formation for AA communities and beyond will be realized.

alienated and segregated from one another. The potential for adhesive cohesion among Asian American communities, when mobilized, is enormous.

To validate the sentiments Dr. Mouw expressed in his charge on Revelation 21, yes, we can imagine all the tribes and tongues to be unified without losing their identity.

Book Reviews

BOOK REVIEW #1

BY **ANAND VEERARAJ**
PRINCETON FORUM ON ASIAN INDIAN MINISTRIES

South Asian Christian Diaspora: Invisible Diaspora in Europe and North America

Kunt A. Jacobsen and Selva J. Raj, eds., *South Asian Christian Diaspora: Invisible Diaspora in Europe and North America* (Burlington, VT: Ashgate Publishing Company, 2008) 284 pp., $99.95, hardcover.

We who serve congregations within ethnic minority immigrant communities are always looking for helpful leadership and ministry resources. When it comes to the South Asian Christian diaspora, such resources are extremely scarce. This need was highlighted at a consultation held at the Princeton Theological Seminary on June 7, 2006. About sixty Asian Indian Pastors and Church leaders from New York, New Jersey and Pennsylvania met together for a consultation on the theme of "Multiplying Asian Indian Ministries in North America." The consultation decided to take steps to address leadership training, and we decided to commence work on an introductory handbook on Asian Indian ministries in North America. We collected and expanded papers presented at the consultation and invited further submissions. Rachel Fell McDermott and I have collaborated to produce the results, the forthcoming anthology, *Pilgrims at the Crossroads: Christians from South Asia at the North American Frontier*.

While working on this anthology, I was introduced to the works of Prema A. Kurien, Syracuse University, Rachel McDermott, Barnard College, New York, Robert Wuthnow, Princeton University, and a few others. These scholars are far ahead in addressing these lacunae in diaspora studies. Prema is a member of my congregation. From time to time, she introduces me to emerging new resources and research in North America. Rachel is also another one of my invaluable informant on such matters.

It is in this context that I was delighted to discover Jacobsen and Raj's *South Asian Christian Diaspora*. The editors themselves claim that this volume "is the first comprehensive study of South Asian Christians living in Europe and North America." One might wish for a truly global perspective, to include regions like East Asia, Australia and New Zealand, but hopefully this work is a step towards such coverage. The editors also have considerably narrowed the scope to fo-

Book Review #1: South Asian Christian Diaspora

cus mainly on the Roman Catholic Tamils from South India and Sri Lanka. Writing in the preface, Knut explains the motive for such a narrow focus as "the almost complete absence of the Roman Catholic Tamils in the research literature on religion in the Sir Lankan and Indian diaspora. It was almost as if they were non-existent. ... They were an invisible diaspora." Indeed, "Making an Invisible Diaspora Visible" has been the driving motivation as stated in the introduction. It is true that to a large extent, Catholic Christians from South Asia are relatively invisible in the overall scheme of South Asian Christian Diasporas. It is in the nature of the Protestant psyche to be loud and drown out competing voices. The project team has sought to overcome this by giving voices to this silent majority and made them come alive. But that choice seems to have limited the usefulness of this book somewhat. Besides, a major part of the book is devoted to the diaspora in Europe while only a few chapters are devoted to the diaspora in North America.

This collection provides many angles from which the South Asian Christian Diaspora in Europe and North America can be perceived and presented. South Asian cultures and religious traditions are pluralistic, colorful and luxurious. It is not a small task to observe and present portrayals of these communities in their multifarious transmutations as supplanted on alien soils. The editors have taken great pains to gather a team of scholars to study and present this phenomenon not only from field studies, but also view them through the prisms of diaspora theories. The volume is made lively with narratives, stories, field surveys and interviews with priest, pastors, the church hierarchy and ordinary lay people confronting the challenges of living on an alien soil. I recommend starting with the concluding chapter, Willams' "South Asian Christians in the West," and then the introduction by the editors, "Making an Invisible Diaspora Visible" before delving into the remaining chapters.

Rachel McDermott was closely associated with this project, contributing an essay on the plight of Dalit Christians (Christians of schedule castes and untouchables) settled in the New York and New Jersey metropolitan region. Her essay was the only one in the volume on this topic. The editors themselves acknowledge the fact that the volume accords "limited coverage and attention . . . to Dalit Christian immigrants even though they constitute the largest segment of the Indian Christian population." Indeed most Christians in North America, including pastors like us, shy away from confronting this "elephant in the room."

I commend Rachel for venturing out where Indian Christians fear to tread.

On a side note, the jacket image — two Tamil Catholic Christian youth bare chested with rosaries around their neck clad in saffron *lungi* (a skirt around the waist) after having performed the tonsure ritual and taken a sacred bath in the ocean in Velankanni (Our Lady of Health), South India — is captivating to say the least. Nevertheless, I would have preferred something similar from either Europe or North America.

Unexpectedly, Selva J. Raj died on 14 March 2008 before he could see the release of this volume. He was at that time serving as the Chair of Religious Studies at Albion College, Michigan, and has published numerous scholarly works on South Asian religious traditions. Rachel was a close friend of Selva and includes a touching tribute to his life and legacy. Selva leaves behind a huge legacy of his passion and works in diaspora studies. That in itself is an open invitation to the scholars and researchers on South Asian Christian diaspora to take up the unfinished task as pioneered and modeled by the life and work of the late Selva J. Raj.

BOOK REVIEW #2

BY **AMOS YONG**
REGENT UNIVERSITY SCHOOL OF DIVINITY, VIRGINIA BEACH, VIRGINIA

Korean American Evangelicals: New Models for Civic Life

Elaine Howard Ecklund, *Korean American Evangelicals: New Models for Civic Life* (Oxford: Oxford University Press, 2006) ix + 211 pp., $22.95, paperback.

This first book is a revision of a Cornell University PhD dissertation in sociology completed in 2004. Ecklund, an Anglo-American and now Assistant Professor of Sociology and Associate Director of the Center on Race, Religion, and Urban Life at Rice University (Houston, Texas), deploys primarily ethnographic and qualitative research methods, especially the interview, in gathering her data. Her interpretations and analyses are laid out in eight chapters in this book.

Chapter 1 introduces the volume, presents the research question – "How do multiethnic and ethnic-specific churches, and the Korean Americans in these churches, connect religion and civic life?" (p. 12) – and suggests the major discovery (thesis) of the volume: "that an individualistic ethic of civic responsibility, such as that found at Manna [the multiethnic congregation focused on by Ecklund] and other multiethnic churches, actually has the ability to promote more volunteering than a collectivist ethic toward volunteering, such as that found at Grace [the ethnic specific congregation studied in detail by Ecklund] and the other Korean American congregations" (p. 13). (Note: church names, of Grace and Manna as well as other congregations included in the study, and of individual interviewee names, are all pseudonyms in the book; all we know is that both churches are located in a modestly sized, not megapolis, urban community in the Northeast part of the country, and it can be gleaned from the narrative that there is at least a local university and seminary in the vicinity.) The second chapter then lays out the various theoretical approaches to the socio-cultural study of the relationship between institutions and identities, and locates Ecklund's own method – that which emphasizes the possible ways in which individuals in institutions have access a wide range of cultural, religious, ideological, ethnic, and other schemas to reconceive for their own purposes – within that broader framework.

The next two chapters introduce both congregations and the models of civic responsibility that operate (mostly implicitly) therein. Grace is an English speaking congregation of second generation Korean Americans who remain closely tied in with the mother church (comprised of first generation Korean immigrants), while Manna is a multiethnic congregation that is constituted primarily by although not limited to Korean and Chinese Americans, is pastored by a Korean couple, includes Anglos and African Americans, and which rents meeting space from an African American church. Needless to say, Grace is dominated by the collectivist mentality prevalent among East Asian cultures, even as its members and adherents continuously struggle to articulate and live out a Christian faith that is both distinctive from that of the mother church while yet also enabling further assimilation into American culture. Manna, on the other hand, is founded on the mantra emphasizing the importance of accepting and appreciating the ethnic and racial diversity of all people made in the image of God, resulting in a rather individualist mentality and ethos. Hence civic life, as the fifth chapter details, is largely organized through the church at Grace, while it is considered the responsibility of members to pursue and work out in accordance to their own calling at Manna. Chapter six thus observes, among other features, how Grace collectively attempts to live up to, even if only implicitly rather than explicitly, the model-minority stereotype often applied to Asian Americans, while Manna in many respects and understandably so, given its multiethnic constituency, rejects that same self-understanding.

The result, perhaps surprisingly, is that while civic volunteerism is organized ecclesially at Grace, fewer of its members are more consistently involved in such activities than at Manna, where civic life is left up the individual members to discern and engage. It appears that people at Manna are more motivated, or at least respond more frequently in measurable forms of civic action, when the ecclesial message is that they are responsible as individuals to seek out and then embody the love of Christ in service to the poor and unfortunate of society. By contrast, the collectivist identity of Grace imposes less urgency on members to volunteer in serving those outside the church: so long as someone shows up for congregationally sponsored service events and activities, the responsibility of the church suffices for its individual members – at least this appears to be the operative logic. Perhaps by extension, Grace's view of political life (the topic of chapter 7) is dominated, when the political registers at all, by the rhetoric and model of the Christian Religious Right, while Manna's approach is much more informed by her relationship with the black church from which she rents meeting space, resulting in a much more progressive socio-political vision. Ecklund concludes somewhat optimistically in her final chapter that given the results of her research, there remain possibilities for Korean American evangelicals to contribute to the transformation of American evangelicalism, as overwhelmingly white as it is.

The strength of Ecklund's thesis is that her control group, second generation Korean American evangelicals, is quite specific. What this volume reveals is that even as narrow a category of ethnic minorities within a fairly circumscribed geographical area and class level (mostly educated and middle to upper middle class socioeconomic status) as researched in this study supports a wide range of civic and even public (political) self-understandings. The theory of cultural schemas illuminates how Grace constituents by and large work within, or even against, the first generation immigrant Korean mentality, while Manna evangelicals are informed by their multiethnic makeup and relationships. Both cases, however, involves re-readings of the Bible from those particular vantage points, producing theological self-characterizations, on the one hand (Grace), to emphasize a more pure or authentic Christianity when measured by the Christian life of their parents, and on the other hand (Manna), to embody the diverse and egalitarian community that values each member as individually created in the image of God. The result is an unpredictability about the trajectories of second generation ethnic evangelicalism and how various groups, each one reflecting a diversity of cultural schemas, might shape, even diversify, the next generation of evangelical discursive practices vis-à-vis civic life.

The volume concludes with two appendices – on data and methods, and on the interview and survey guides used in the study – and notes and references. While Ecklund's own analyses are a bit repetitive after the laying out of the book's thesis in the first chapter, what keeps the book interesting are the rich perspectives of Korean American evangelicals preserved in their own words in this book. Herein we find solid sociological research enlivened by real lives, views, concerns, and hopes. Since the publication of this volume Ecklund appears to have turned her gaze more intentionally in other directions – e.g., witness the appearance of her *Science vs Religion: What Do Scientists Really Think?* (Oxford University Press, 2010). Yet even if that is the case, her book Korean American Evangelicals remains replete with insights regarding and fruitful research trajectories for a range of topics: Asian American studies, Asian American evangelicalism, or ethnic minority studies in general.

BOOK REVIEW #3

BY **RUSSELL JEUNG**
SAN FRANCISCO STATE UNIVERSITY

A Faith of Our Own: Second Generation Spirituality in Korean American Churches

Sharon Kim, *A Faith of Our Own: Second Generation Spirituality in Korean American Churches* (New Brunswick, NJ: Rutgers University Press, 2010) ix + 200 pp., $23.95, paperback.

Sharon Kim's sociological analysis, *A Faith of Our Own*, is a colorful and compelling account of the entrepreneurial movement and creative energies of second generation Korean American churches in the Los Angeles area. Well-documented and interestingly written, it demonstrates how these congregations have hybridized American and Korean spiritual practices to develop their own unique, religious institutions.

This comprehensive study, based on ethnographic work of 22 churches and interviews with 108 ministers and church leaders, details: 1) why these Korean American congregations have formed; 2) what religious traditions and spiritual resources they emphasize; 3) how they engage with the outside community; and 4) how they identify ethnically and racially. Kim cogently argues that these spaces are not simply sanctuaries from racial marginalization or from their parents' traditionalism, but are living laboratories of singularly American, incipient faith practices.

Like other Asian American congregations and ministries, these churches developed in response to ethnic and racial factors. Ethnic, generational tensions spurred the second generation ministers to plant independent churches. One powerful illustration of such differences described in the book involved conflicting perspectives on careers. At one church revival meeting, almost half the college attendees made commitments to give up their careers for full-time ministry. The parents complained to the leadership of the church, and coerced most of the students to pursue more upwardly mobile occupations. Kim tempers criticisms of immigrant churches, though, and does identify strengths of these congregations as well.

Similarly, the second generation did not feel comfortable within mainstream churches, either. Kim's respondents did not face behavioral discrimination, but perceived attitudinal prejudices that made them feel unwelcome at other churches. Within Korean American congregations, on the other hand, they felt at home with others with similar upbringings and values. Why Korean Americans, more than other Asian American ethnic groups, seek to maintain their ethnic identities and associations in churches could be further explored. Nonetheless, the religious and social motivations provided in the book do resonate.

What I found most interesting were the elements that characterize these new churches. Not surprisingly, they utilize contemporary American Christian worship styles and leadership principles to run their churches. However, ministers consciously and strategically promote Korean prayer rituals, such as *tongsongkido* (unison prayer). These rituals involve much emotional fervor, which the ministers claim are more authentic and effective ways for Christians to pray than found at mainstream churches.

Another Asian spiritual value that these ministers actively espouse is collectivism. In challenging excessive American individualism, the congregations seek to build biblical communities in which members' commitments and responsibilities are predicated on the serving their church rather than their own self-interests. As one example, Kim relates how one pastor's first sermon for his new church was entitled, "The Declaration of Interdependence," to emphasize the priority of community in this church plant. He said that in his Korean American upbringing, he was taught to think of family before himself. He reads the Bible in the same way, considering God's word to the group more than to each individual's personal concerns.

One final, striking feature of second generation Korean American congregations is their renunciation of materialism and call for compassion and social justice. Eighteen of the twenty-two congregations sponsored some sort of social service, "compassion ministry," and 61% of the members in these congregations indicated that they had invested time or money in these projects. Kim describes several examples of these ministries in attempts to combat complaints that Korean churches are too insular.

So, what does the future hold for these congregations? While these ministers predominantly want to develop multiracial churches, they remain largely pan-Asian churches drawing other Asian ethnic groups. Replicating findings from my research and others, *A Faith of Our Own* shows that racial dynamics continue to shape the trajectories of churches in the United States.

Kim has a well-balanced view of these congregations as she identifies the strengths and weaknesses of ethnic, pan-ethnic, and multiracial models of congregations. I personally wanted to learn more about the hybridization process, and how other ethnic American congregations might contextualize their cultural and racial experiences within the church. Kim admits that second generation spirituality is still a young project, far from being fully realized. Nonetheless, her insider, sanguine perspective provides glimpses of how Asian American churches can bless the larger church body and our nation as well.

BOOK REVIEW #4

BY **URIAH Y. KIM**
HARTFORD SEMINARY

They were All Together in One Place? Toward Minority Biblical Criticism

Randall C. Bailey, Tat-siong Benny Liew, and Fernando F. Segovia (eds.), *They were All Together in One Place? Toward Minority Biblical Criticism* (Atlanta: Society of Biblical Literature, 2009) xiv + 397pp., $45.95, paperback.

The editors in their introductory essay, "Toward Minority Biblical Criticism: Framework, Contours, Dynamics," celebrate the coming together of scholars from three minority groups in the U.S., namely, African Americans, Asian Americans, and Latino/a Americans, to speak among themselves about what is and how to do minority biblical criticism. There are two primary audiences to which this volume speaks: minority biblical scholars and people who are actively engaged in ethnic/racial minority Christian communities. White Americans and scholars are still present in this volume, casting a shadow no minority group can ever escape in North America, but they are not the primary audience as so often is in writings of minority scholars. There is a strong sense of accomplishment in the introductory article. Indeed it must have been difficult to launch and finish this project and to gather these scholars so that they can talk to one another and to move toward an undertaking of spreading the message of doing minority biblical criticism. They are not shy about explicating their intention to form a coalition or an alliance among minority scholars to transform the discipline of biblical studies and in the process change the way all Christians read and interpret the Bible. They make clear that it is the common experience being treated as 'minority' in the U.S. that becomes the hermeneutical lens through which interpreting the text is practiced in minority biblical criticism.

I must admit that the term 'minority' really bothers me. It is not a neutral word in the context of the U.S. society where 'minority' groups are often treated like second-class citizens. It sounds as if those who are labeled 'minority' as being somehow inadequate, insufficient, or even immature in comparison to the dominant group. The editors rightly qualify this term but do so in the preface of the book rather than in their introductory article. They explain that "minority" should include the meaning of "minoritization" or "the process of unequal valorization of population groups," and the term is used throughout the book to point out "this demeaning practice" and "to challenge, contest, or change the term's meaning" (p. xi). It is a strategy that turns a given negative term on its head into an empowering term, for example, "queer" or "black" theology. The editors also desire that the practice of minority biblical criticism "can turn the undeniable power differential that they [minorities] suffer into springboards for new interpretations and critical interventions" (p. 7).

The essays in this volume are divided into four sections. There are six articles in the first section, "Puncturing Objectivity and Universality," which disrupts the notion that the dominant biblical hermeneutics interprets the text with "objectivity and universality." In fact all articles in the volume in one way or another use the context as point of entry into the reading the text and shatter the pretension of those who claim that their contexts have no bearing on their interpretations. The second section, "Expanding the Field," has only one article and tries "to push aside and move past the established boundaries of the discipline" (p. 28). There is one article in the third section, "Problematizing Criticism," which questions those who seek the "truth" by bounding their inquiries within "disciplinary ideals of detachment and disengagement and unencumbered by social-cultural ties and interests of any sort" (p. 31). In the fourth section, "Taking the Interdisciplinary Turn," three articles pursue "sustained and systematic critical dialogue with scholarly discourses having to do with the problematic of identity" (p. 34). Then follows three essays written by those outside the guild of biblical scholars, assessing significances of the work; the concluding essay is by Segovia who acknowledges that much work is still needed in developing minority biblical criticism in the future but much has been accomplished in this volume and he confidently calls this venture "groundbreaking." Finally, it does not have indices. I think it would have been helpful to have Author, Subject, and Scriptures indices.

There is no question that the essays in this volume deal with critical issues relevant to Asian American Christianity: how race/ethnicity, sex/gender, and socioeconomic concerns matter in interpreting the Bible. It is also certain that most authors in this volume take "progressive" approach or stance. This does not mean that those who are more inclined to a traditional, conservative, or evangelical leaning should ignore or discount this work. All Asian American Christians will find this volume stimulating, insightful, provocative, and relevant to their faith and understanding of the Bible. In the following I will review only the articles written by Asian Americans so that I can deal with them in greater detail than if I had reviewed all articles. By this I am not suggesting that the essays written by African-American and Latino/a American scholars are not as important to Asian American Christianity as those written by Asian Americans.

Frank M. Yamada, who teaches at McCormack Theological Seminary, reflects on an issue and event all Asian Americans should be aware of in "What Does Manzanar Have to Do with Eden? A Japanese American Interpretation of Genesis 2-3" (pp. 97-117). Yamada reads Genesis 2-3 with the historical experience of the Japanese interment of World War II in the Unites States when the Japanese and Japanese American people "were imprisoned solely on the basis of race and ethnicity without due process of law" (p. 103). He argues that the exercise of God's authority in the story reveals Yahweh's anxious desire to maintain the division between the human and divine realms just as the exercise of authority by the U.S. government was for the purpose of self-preservation in light of a perceived threat from the other, in this case, Americans of Japanese descent. For many Japanese Americans the choice was between compliance in the form of imprisonment or further punishment for noncooperation just as the human beings' choice was limited to a yes or no to the divine imperative while being under suspicion. He makes an interesting observation that the human beings (earthlings) in the Genesis story do not die on the day they disobey God's command. In fact they continue to survive, albeit outside of the garden just as Japanese Americans survived the life of adversity during the interment and even thrived afterwards.

Gale A. Yee, who teaches at Episcopal Divinity School, reflects on two stereotypes all Asian Americans deal with in "'She Stood in Tears Amid the Alien Corn': Ruth, the Perpetual Foreigner and Model Minority" (pp. 119-140). Yee examines the portrayal of Asian Americans in general and Chinese Americans in particular as the "perpetual foreigner" and "model minority" as a strategy of the dominant group both to exploit them as second-class citizens in their own land and to use them as a propagandistic tool to support the dominant ideology of the U.S. as a just and fair society and to punish and/or put to shame other minorities for complaining about the state of U.S. society. She argues that the double and contradictory portrayal can shed light on understanding a similarly two-sided interpretation of Ruth the Moabite. She first notes that "the usual optimistic and romantic readings of Ruth obscure issues of ethnicity, economic exploitation, and racist attitudes about the sexuality of foreigners are evident in the text" (p. 127). This reading sees Ruth not only as the model convert but also an exemplar for the Jewish people; she epitomizes the concept of hesed (loyalty and kindness) for the people of Israel. Yee highlights the fact that just as Ruth the Moabite "teaches Judeans the meaning of hesed, Asian Americans educate Others on how to be "good" minorities who knows their place in a white society" (p. 130). Ruth the Moabite, however, is not fully accepted as one of their own. The fact that she is labeled as a Moabite throughout the book, she is like Asian Americans in the U.S., "not fully assimilated in the text's consciousness of what it means to be Israelite" (p. 133)-the perpetual foreigner. She concludes that Ruth's story is "an indictment for those of us who live in the First World who exploit the cheap labor of developing countries and poor immigrants from these countries who come to the First World looking for jobs" (p. 134).

Jae Won Lee, who teaches at McCormick Theological Seminary, questions the assumption that there are no ethnic concerns in Paul's writing in "Paul and Ethnic Differences in Romans" (pp. 141-157). Lee notes that many people believe that ethnic concerns are matters important for a few ethnic scholars but are irrelevant to those scholars interested in normative, historical, objective, value-free criticism. She raises this issue in her examination of Paul's politics of differences in Romans 14-15 by showing that the discourse about the "strong" and the "weak" in Romans is among the earliest cases of the "us versus them" construction based on ethnic particularity in early Christian groups. She critiques the biblical criticism utilized by those who don't pay attention to ethnic concerns by arguing that the hermeneutics of the "strong" (dominant biblical criticism) dominates the hermeneutics of the "weak" (minority biblical criticism) "while disguising its exclusive tendency, that is, the hegemony of identity, in its claim for universality" (p. 144).

Tat-siong Benny Liew teaches at Pacific School of Religion. In his article, "Queering Closets and Perverting Desires: Cross-Examining John's Engendering and Trans-gendering Word Across Different Worlds" (pp. 251-288), perhaps the most provocative article in the entire volume, Liew raises an issue of not seeing or covering up what is in the text for the sake of one's ideology. Liew attempts to show that there are "signs" of concerns for race/ethnicity and sexuality in the text of John, leading to a view that Jesus is depicted as a transvestite. He clarifies that he is not claiming that John's Jesus is "really" a female, an androgyny, or a "failed" man but that the male and/or female identity is illegible. He calls for readers of John "to analyze and perhaps even challenge the discursive and material forces that discipline one's acts, practices, and identities" (p. 260) and hopes to redress "the wrongs that have been suffered by people who have not been gendered strictly as either male or female" (p. 261).

James Kyung-Jin Lee teaches Asian American studies and English at the University of California, Santa Barbara. His article, "The Difference that Damage Makes: Reflections of an Ethnic Studies Scholar on the Wabash Consultation" (pp. 347-362) reflects on a yearning I believe many Asian Americans experienced. In assessing the volume Lee articulates "the desire to see oneself in another." He sees this desire as "an ethical response to the condition of alienation that perhaps is a mark of anyone's fundamental humanity but that those geographically displaced, culturally unmoored, and spiritually detached fell most acutely" (p. 348).

For some time now Asian American biblical scholars have been reflecting and writing on promises and predicaments, advantages and disadvantages of being Asian Americans in North America, but now they are engaging with other minority groups to force all interpreters of the Bible to take account of their contexts in their readings of the Bible. As Asian American Christians we tend to focus on personal piety or transformation when we read and interpret the Bible, but this volume challenges us that when we interpret the Bible we cannot afford to ignore social, cultural, political, and theological forces that continue to minoritize and racialize us as second-class citizens or Christians in North America.

Manuscript Submission Guidelines

The SANACS Journal encourages and welcomes submissions that advance the Journal's mission to disseminate scholarly studies of Asian North American Christianity.

Submissions are evaluated by a blind jury of qualified academic specialists. The current jury of seventeen scholars are divided into six groups: Bible, Theology, Missiology, History, Sociology, and Praxis, though interdisciplinary studies are welcome as well.

The SANACS journal also publishes book, media, and exhibition reviews, though these are not jury reviewed. Note that the SANACS journal does not solicit works focused on Christianity in Asia (unless explicitly relating to Asian North American Christianity) or works written by Asian North American scholars but lacking explicit attention to Asian North American Christianity.

Since submissions are blind reviewed, authors need not possess particular academic degrees ranks, or appointments. However, all works should have a clearly academic focus that appropriately engages other scholarly literature. Works that appear in the Journal identify authors only by name and institutional affiliation(s), and without degrees or titles.

Works need not be otherwise unpublished, but previously published works would have to be evaluated for appropriateness and availability before being considered. Please inform us if your submission has been previously published.

Submissions may include charts and pictures, but these should be clearly essential to the work. Any necessary permissions are the responsibility of the author.

Please submit your work as an email attachment in Microsoft Word format (*.doc, not *docx; and not as a *.pdf.). Please use standard formatting (double spaced, one inch margins, 12-point Times New Roman font for the body text).

We encourage footnotes rather than endnotes. However, for literature citations, we encourage short form (author and year) with a full endnote bibliography of works cited. (This simplifies formatting for publication.) However we know some submissions may have already been formatted with long citations in the footnotes and will try to accommodate this.

Please help our blind review process by submitting your work thusly: your name should appear only on a cover page (could even be a separate 1-page

Manuscript Submission Guidelines

document), which the jurors will not see. Your submission proper should be anonymous, without your identity as the author appearing in any noticeable way.

Please also include at the top of the paper itself an approximately 100-word abstract following the title page to help the Journal assign submissions to jury members. Articles should generally not exceed thirty (30) word-processed, double-spaced pages, excluding end matter.

Please send submissions to:

Russell Yee, Managing Editor, SANACS Journal

ryee@isaacweb.org.

If it is necessary send anything hard copy (including books for notice or review) please send to:

Russell Yee

4044 La Cresta Avenue

Oakland, CA 94602-1731

We will acknowledge the receipt of your work and try to make an editorial decision within fifteen weeks of its arrival. Please feel free to inquire as to the appropriateness of possible submissions, especially works in progress.